Texas Rangers 2019

A Baseball Companion

Edited by Patrick Dubuque, Aaron Gleeman and Bret Sayre

Baseball Prospectus

Craig Brown and Dave Pease, Consultant Editors
Rob McQuown and Harry Pavlidis, Statistics Editors

Copyright © 2019 by DIY Baseball, LLC.
All rights reserved

This book or any part thereof may not be reproduced or transmitted in any form or by any means, electronic or mechanical, including photocopying, recording, or by any information storage and retrieval system, without permission in writing from the publisher.

Limit of Liability/Disclaimer of Warranty: While the publisher and the author have used their best efforts in preparing this book, they make no representations or warranties with respect to the accuracy or completeness of the contents of this book and specifically disclaim any implied warranties of merchantability or fitness for a particular purpose. No warranty may be created or extended by sales representatives or written sales materials. The advice and strategies contained herein may not be suitable for your situation. You should consult with a professional where appropriate. Neither the publisher nor the author shall be liable for any loss of profit or any other commercial damages, including but not limited to special, incidental, consequential, or other damages.

Library of Congress Cataloging-in-Publication Data:
paperback
ISBN-13: 978-1-949332-26-1

Project Credits
Cover Design: Kathleen Dyson
Interior Design and Production: Jeff Pease, Dave Pease
Layout: Jeff Pease, Dave Pease

Baseball icon courtesy of Uberux, from https://www.shareicon.net/author/uberux

Ballpark diagram courtesy of Lou Spirito/THIRTY81 Project, https://thirty81project.com/

Manufactured in the United States of America
10 9 8 7 6 5 4 3 2 1

Table of Contents

Foreword v
    Rob Mains

Statistical Introduction vii

Part 1: Team Analysis

Table for Three: Previewing the 2019 Texas Rangers 3
    Aaron Gleeman, Tim McCullough and Kate Morrison

Performance Graphs 7

2018 Team Performance 8

2019 Team Projections 9

Team Personnel 10

Globe Life Park in Arlington Stats 11

Rangers Team Analysis 13

Part 2: Player Analysis

Rangers Player Analysis 18

Rangers Prospects 101

Part 3: Featured Articles

The Hole in The Shift is Fixing Itself 117
    Russell Carleton

The State of the Quality Start 121
    Rob Mains

Heads-Up Hacking—The First Pitch 127
    Matthew Trueblood

A Hymn for the Index Stat 133
    Patrick Dubuque

Index of Names 137

Foreword

Rob Mains

Welcome to this companion of the 2019 Texas Rangers. We at Baseball Prospectus are excited to provide this analysis of the Rangers.

Our website, Baseball Prospectus, is a leader in delivering high-quality commentary and data to baseball fans everywhere. To some, those words—commentary and data—appear mutually exclusive. There are people out there who believe that traditional analysis and advanced analytics must run on different paths. But the simplistic narrative of stats vs. traditionalists just isn't true. Every team's analytics department interacts with scouting, development, and major league operations with a common goal: Delivering a championship. New technologies, like radar tracking of pitch speeds and movement, enable talent evaluators to focus on qualitative aspects of pitching like mechanics and pitch sequencing. In-game strategies like infield shifts, based on batters' hit tendencies, help turn balls in play into outs. Hitters use information to adjust their swings to maximize run production.

All these numbers can seem, at best, intimidating, and at worst, counterproductive to the casual fan. Even as technology and analysis have embedded themselves deeply into the way teams run, it can often feel like statistics create a displacement between the viewer and the sport, breaking them out of the action. And yet every fan incorporates the numbers to some degree; stats like batting average and earned run average, so fundamental to how we talk about performance, are actually complicated formulas. They don't bother people because those formulas have become second nature, as easy to translate as the action on the field.

Along the way, new statistics have entered baseball's lexicon. You'll see some of them, like on-base percentage (which measures a batter's ability to get on base via walk, hit batter, or hit), OPS (on-base plus slugging), and average exit velocity (the speed of balls off a hitter's bat) on broadcasts. Others, like DRC+, might well be new to you. Some of them have been well-defined to the public, others haven't. That lack of context has created ambiguity. Fans know that a ball hit 100 mph is scorched, but does that mean extra bases? (Not if it's hit on the ground or high in the air it doesn't.)

For those who are amenable to them, the new statistics can increase the enjoyment and understanding of the game. They can help fans identify when a pitcher is tiring, when a stolen base or a bunt attempt makes sense (and, more often, when it doesn't), or how a team's lineup might be constructed. Websites like Baseball Prospectus add to that understanding by weaving metrics into the narrative of the game. That's the goal of this publication: to take some of the newer, more complicated statistics and make them as intuitive as the ones on the back of old baseball cards.

But you don't need to love analytics to love baseball. The fans at BP who worked together to write this guide are captivated first and foremost by the game itself. We're drawn to Aaron Judge's power, Francisco Lindor's glove, Billy Hamilton's speed and Patrick Corbin's slider and don't need numbers to tell us why they're so mesmerizing. The underlying statistics provide depth to the game that we all love.

We hope you'll find that this guide helps you better understand the Rangers. Our analysts have studied the team's major league personnel and its minor league affiliates to identify their strengths and weaknesses, both the obvious ones and those that only a careful dissection of players' performances—yes, including the data—can reveal. You don't need us to tell you who was good and who wasn't in 2018, but our models and writers can help you project how each player is going to perform this year and beyond, and appreciate the greatness of each new game as it unfolds. As in the sport itself, the human and analytic components combine to generate a deeper overall understanding.

Think back to the first time you saw a baseball game on a high-definition TV. You'd grown familiar with how the game looked and felt on a picture tube. But new TV allowed you to see details that you'd never seen before. That's how advanced statistics work. The game itself is why you're here and why you're buying this. (And, for that matter, why we wrote it.) The statistical measures provide the sharper focus, the detail, the depth of knowledge that you didn't have before, generating an overall superior picture. Enjoy the view.

—*Rob Mains is an author of Baseball Prospectus.*

Statistical Introduction

Sports are, fundamentally, a blend of athletic endeavor and storytelling. Baseball, like any other sport, tells its stories in so many ways: in the arc of a game from the stands or a season from the box scores, in photos, or even in numbers. At Baseball Prospectus, we understand that statistics don't replace observation or any of baseball's stories, but complement everything else that makes the game so much fun.

What stats help us with is with patterns and precision, variance and value. This book can help you learn things you may not see from watching a game or hundred, whether it's the path of a career over time or the breadth of the entire MLB. We'd also never ask you to choose between our numbers and the experience of viewing a game from the cheap seats or the comfort of your home; our publication combines running the numbers with observations and wisdom from some of the brightest minds we can find. But if you *do* want to learn more about the numbers beyond what's on the backs of player jerseys, let us help explain.

Offense

At the end of this past year, we've revised our methodology for determining batting value. Long-time readers of Baseball Prospectus will notice that we've retired True Average in favor of a new metric: Deserved Runs Created Plus (DRC+). Developed by Jonathan Judge and our stats team, this statistic measures everything a player does at the plate–reaching base, hitting for power, making outs, and moving runners over–and puts it on a scale where 100 equals league-average performance. A DRC+ of 150 is terrific, a DRC+ of 100 is average, and a DRC+ of 75 means you better be an excellent defender.

DRC+ also does a better job than any of our previous metrics in taking contextual factors into account. The model adjusts for how the park affects performance, but also for things like the talent of the opposing pitcher, value of different types of batted-ball events, league, temperature, and other factors. It's able to describe a player's expected offensive contribution than any other statistic we've found over the years, and also does a better job of predicting future performance as well.

The other aspect of run-scoring is baserunning, which we quantify using Baserunning Runs. BRR not only records the value of stolen bases (or getting caught in the act), but also accounts for a runner's ability to go first to third on a single or advance on a fly ball.

Defense

Where offensive value is *relatively* easy to identify and understand, defensive value is … not. Over the past dozen years, the sabermetric community has focused mostly on stats based on zone data: a real-live human person records the type of batted ball and estimated landing location, and models are created that give expected outs. From there, you can compare fielders' actual outs to those expected ones. Simple, right?

Unfortunately, zone data has two major issues. First, zone data is recorded by commercial data providers who keep the raw data private unless you pay for it. (All the statistics we build in this book and on our website use public data as inputs.) That hurts our ability to test assumptions or duplicate results. Second, over the years it has become apparent that there's quite a bit of "noise" in zone-based fielding analysis. Sometimes the conclusions drawn from zone data don't hold up to scrutiny, and sometimes the different data provided by different providers don't look anything alike, giving wildly different results. Sometimes the hard-working professional stringers or scorers might unknowingly inflict unconscious bias into the mix: for example good fielders will often be credited with more expected outs despite the data, and ballparks with high press boxes tend to score more line drives than ones with a lower press box.

Enter our Fielding Runs Above Average (FRAA). For most positions, FRAA is built from play-by-play data, which allows us to avoid the subjectivity found in many other fielding metrics. The idea is this: count how many fielding plays are made by a given player and compare that to expected plays for an average fielder at their position (based on pitcher ground-ball tendencies and batter handedness). Then we adjust for park and base-out situations.

When it comes to catchers, our methodology is a little different thanks to the laundry list of responsibilities they're tasked with beyond just, well, catching and throwing the ball. By now you've probably heard about "framing" or the art of making umpires more likely to call balls outside the strike zone for strikes. To put this into one tidy number, we incorporate pitch tracking data (for the years it exists) and adjust for important factors like pitcher, umpire, batter, and home-field advantage using a mixed-model approach. This grants us a number for how many strikes the catcher is personally adding to (or subtracting from) his pitchers' performance … which we then convert to runs added or lost using linear weights.

Framing is one of the biggest parts of determining catcher value, but we also take into account blocking balls from going past, whether a scorer deems it a passed ball or a wild pitch. We use a similar approach–one that really benefits from the pitch tracking data that tells us what ends up in the dirt and what doesn't. We also include a catcher's ability to prevent stolen bases and how well they field balls in play, and *finally* we come up with our FRAA for catchers.

Pitching

Both pitching and fielding make up the half of baseball that isn't run scoring: run prevention. Separating pitching from fielding is a tough task, and most recent pitching analysis has branched off from Voros McCracken's famous (and controversial) statement, "There is little if any difference among major-league pitchers in their ability to prevent hits on balls hit in the field of play." The research of the analytic community has validated this to some extent, and there are a host of "defense-independent" pitching measures that have been developed to try and extricate the effect of the defense behind a hurler from the pitcher's work.

Our solution to this quandry is Deserved Run Average (DRA), our core pitching metric. DRA looks like earned run average (ERA), the tried-and-true pitching stat you've seen on every baseball broadcast or box score from the past century, but it's very different. To start, DRA takes an event-by-event look at what the pitchers does, and adjusts the value of that event based on different environmental factors like park, batter, catcher, umpire, base-out situation, run differential, inning, defense, home field advantage, pitcher role, and temperature. That mixed model gives us a pitcher's expected contribution, similar to what we do for our DRC+ model for hitters and FRAA model for catchers. (Oh, and we also consider the pitcher's effect on basestealing and on balls getting past the catcher.)

It's important to note that DRA is set to the scale of runs allowed per nine innings (RA9) instead of ERA, which makes DRA's scale slightly higher than ERA's. The reason for this is because ERA tends to overrate three types of pitchers:

1. Pitchers who play in parks where scorers hand out more errors. Official scorers differ significantly in the frequency at which they assign errors to fielders.
2. Ground-ball pitchers, because a substantial proportion of errors occur on grounders.
3. Pitchers who aren't very good. Better pitchers often allow fewer unearned runs than bad pitchers, because good pitchers tend to find ways to get out of jams.

Since the last time you picked up an edition of this book, we've also made a few minor changes to DRA to make it better. Recent research into "tunneling"–the act of throwing consecutive pitches that appear similar from a batter's point of view until after the swing decision point–data has given us a new contextual factor to account for in DRA: plate distance. This refers to the distance between successive pitches as they approach the plate, and while it has a smaller effect than factors like velocity or whiff rate, it still can help explain pitcher strikeout rate in our model.

New Pitching Metrics for 2019

We're including a few "new" pitching metrics for 2019's suite of Baseball Prospectus publications, but you may be familiar with them if you've spent time scouring the internet for stats.

Fastball Percentage

Our fastball percentage (FB%) statistic measures how frequently a pitcher throws a pitch classified as a "fastball," measured as a percentage of overall pitches thrown. We qualify three types of fastballs:

1. The traditional four-seam fastball;
2. The two-seam fastball or sinker;
3. "Hard cutters," which are pitches that have the movement profile of a cut fastball and are used as the pitcher's primary offering or in place of a more traditional fastball.

For example, a pitcher with a FB% of 67 throws any combination of these three pitches about two-thirds of the time.

Whiff Rate

Everybody loves a swing and a miss, and whiff rate (WHF) measures how frequently pitchers induce a swinging strike. To calculate WHF, we add up all the pitches thrown that ended with a swinging strike, then divide that number by a pitcher's total pitches thrown. Most often, high whiff rates correlate with high strikeout rates (and overall effective pitcher performance).

Called Strike Probability

Called Strike Probability (CSP) is a number that represents the likelihood that all of a pitcher's pitches will be called a strike while controlling for location, pitcher and batter handedness, umpire and count. Here's how it works: on each pitch, our model determines how many times (out of 100) that a similar pitch was called for a strike given those factors mentioned above, and when normalized for each batter's strike zone. Then we average the CSP for all pitches thrown by a pitcher in a season, and that gives us the yearly CSP percentage you see in the stats boxes.

As you might imagine, pitchers with a higher CSP are more likely to work in the zone, where pitchers with a lower CSP are likely locating their pitches outside the normal strike zone, for better or for worse.

Projections

Many of you aren't turning to this book just for a look at what a player has done, but for a look at what a player is going to do: the PECOTA projections. PECOTA, initially developed by Nate Silver (who has moved on to greater fame as a political analyst), consists of three parts:

1. Major-league equivalencies, which use minor-league statistics to project how a player will perform in the major leagues;
2. Baseline forecasts, which use weighted averages and regression to the mean to estimate a player's current true talent level; and
3. Aging curves, which uses the career paths of comparable players to estimate how a player's statistics are likely to change over time.

With all those important things covered, let's take a look at what's in the book this year.

Team Prospectus

You bought this book to learn more about your favorite (or maybe least-favorite, who are we to judge?) team, so let's talk about them. After a thoughtful preview of the 2019 season, you'll be presented with our Team Prospectus. This outlines many of the key statistics for each team's 2018 season, as well as a very inviting stadium diagram.

First you'll find the Performance Graphs page. The first is the 2018 Hit List Ranking. This shows our Hit List Rank for the team on each day of the 2018 season and is intended to give you a picture of the ups and downs of the team's season, including their highest and lowest ranks of the year. Hit List Rank measures overall team performance and drives the Hit List Power Rankings at the baseballprospectus.com website.

The second graph is Committed Payroll and helps you see how the team's payroll has compared to the MLB and divisional average payrolls over time. Payroll figures are currents as of January 1, 2019; with so many free agents still unsigned as of this writing, the final 2018 figure will likely be significantly different for many teams. (In the meantime, you can always find the most current data at Baseball Prospectus' Cot's Baseball Contracts page.)

The third graph is Farm System Ranking and displays how the Baseball Prospectus prospect team has ranked the organization's farm system since 2007. It also indicates the highest and lowest ranks that the farm system achieved over that time.

We start the Team Performance page with the squad's unadjusted and third-order 2018 win-loss records, presented in divisional context. We then list the three highest performing hitters and pitchers by WARP for 2018. Beneath that are a host of other team statistics. **Pythag** presents an adjusted 2018 winning percentage, calculated by taking runs scored per game (**RS/G**) and runs allowed per game (**RA/G**) for the team, and running them through a version of Bill James' Pythagorean formula that was refined and improved by David Smyth and Brandon Heipp. (The formula is called "Pythagenpat," which is equally fun to type and to say.)

Next up is **DRC+**, described earlier, to indicate the overall hitting ability of the team either above or below league-average. Run prevention on the pitching side is covered by **DRA** (also mentioned earlier) and another metric: Fielding Independent Pitching (**FIP**), which calculates another ERA-like statistic based on strikeouts, walks, and home runs recorded. Defensive Efficiency Rating (**DER**) tells us the percentage of balls in play turned into outs for the team, and is a quick fielding shorthand that rounds out run prevention.

After that, we have several measures related to roster composition, as opposed to on-field performance. **B-Age** and **P-Age** tell us the average age of a team's batters and pitchers, respectively. **Salary** is the combined team payroll for all on-field players, and Doug Pappas' Marginal Dollars per Marginal Win (**M$/MW**) tells us how much money a team spent to earn production above replacement level.

Ending this batch of statistics is the number of disabled list days a team had over the season (**DL Days**) and the amount of salary paid to players on the disabled list (**$ on DL**); this final number is expressed as a percentage of total payroll.

Next to each of these stats, we've listed each team's MLB rank in that category from 1st to 30th. In this, 1st always indicates a positive outcome and 30th a negative outcome, except in the case of salary–1st is highest.

The Team Projections page is intended to convey the team's operational capacity entering the 2019 season. We start with the team's PECOTA projected record for 2019, again in divisional context. The **+/-** column indicates how many more or less wins the team is projected to get than they got in 2018. We then list the three highest projected hitters and pitchers by WARP for 2018. A brief farm system summary follows, with the team's top prospect and number of BP Top 101 Prospects. Finally, we list the key new players and departed players, along with their 2019 projected WARP.

www.baseballprospectus.com

Alex Bregman 3B

Born: 03/30/94 Age: 25 Bats: R Throws: R
Height: 6'0" Weight: 180 Origin: Round 1, 2015 Draft (#2 overall)

YEAR	TEAM	LVL	AGE	PA	R	2B	3B	HR	RBI	BB	K	SB	CS	AVG/OBP/SLG
2016	CCH	AA	22	285	54	16	2	14	46	42	26	5	3	.297/.415/.559
2016	FRE	AAA	22	83	17	6	0	6	15	5	12	2	1	.333/.373/.641
2016	HOU	MLB	22	217	31	13	3	8	34	15	52	2	0	.264/.313/.478
2017	HOU	MLB	23	626	88	39	5	19	71	55	97	17	5	.284/.352/.475
2018	HOU	MLB	24	705	105	51	1	31	103	96	85	10	4	.286/.394/.532
2019	HOU	MLB	25	675	96	38	3	23	78	73	107	12	4	.272/.359/.463

Breakout: 6%   Improve: 52%   Collapse: 5%   Attrition: 2%   MLB: 100%
Comparables: Anthony Rendon, David Wright, Pablo Sandoval

YEAR	TEAM	LVL	AGE	PA	DRC+	VORP	BABIP	BRR	FRAA	WARP
2016	CCH	AA	22	285	172	38.9	.286	1.6	SS(51): -3.4, 3B(11): 1.4	2.7
2016	FRE	AAA	22	83	161	10.0	.333	-1.2	SS(14): 2.1, LF(3): -0.1	0.8
2016	HOU	MLB	22	217	107	9.6	.317	0.5	3B(40): 0.9, SS(6): -0.1	1.1
2017	HOU	MLB	23	626	114	34.7	.311	-1.5	3B(132): 8.7, SS(30): -2.9	3.9
2018	HOU	MLB	24	705	150	72.6	.289	-1.6	3B(136): 5.4, SS(28): -0.4	7.4
2019	HOU	MLB	25	675	125	37.3	.295	0.0	3B 7, SS 0	4.6

After the projections page, we share a few items about the team's home ballpark. There's the aforementioned diagram of the park's dimensions (including distances to the outfield wall), a few important biographical facts about the stadium, a graphic showing the height of the wall from the left-field pole to the right-field pole, and a table showing three-year park factors for the stadium. The park factors are displayed as indexes where 100 is average, 110 means that the park inflates the statistic in question by 10 percent, and 90 means that the park deflates the statistic in question by 10 percent.

Following the ballpark page, we have a **Personnel** section that lists many of the important decision-makers and upper-level field and operations staff members for the franchise, as well as any former Baseball Prospectus staff members who are currently part of the organization.

Position Players

After all that information and a thoughtful bylined essay covering each team, we present our player comments. Each player is listed with the major-league team who employed him as of early January 2019. If a player changed teams after that point via free agency, trade, or any other method, you'll be able to find them in the book for their previous squad.

First, we cover biographical information (age is as of June 30, 2019) before moving onto the stats themselves. Our statistic columns include standard identifying information like **YEAR**, **TEAM**, **LVL** (level of affiliated play) and **AGE** before getting into the numbers. Next, we provide raw, unstranslated numbers like you might find on the back of your dad's baseball cards: **PA** (plate appearances), **R** (runs), **2B** (doubles), **3B** (triples), **HR** (home runs), **RBI** (runs batted in), **BB** (walks), **K** (strikeouts), **SB** (stolen bases) and **CS** (caught stealing). Then we have unadjusted "slash" statistics: **AVG** (batting average), **OBP** (on-base percentage) and **SLG** (slugging percentage).

Just below the stats box is **PECOTA** data, which is discussed further in a following section. After that, it's on to a pithy and always-informative comment written by a member of the Baseball Prospectus staff, before we cover more stats.

The second text box repeats YEAR, TEAM, LVL, AGE, and PA, then moves on to **DRC+** (Deserved Runs Created Plus), which we described earlier as total offensive expected contribution compared to the league average. Next, one of our oldest active metrics, **VORP** (Value Over Replacement Player), considers offensive production, position and plate appearances. In essence, it is the number of runs contributed beyond what a replacement-level player at the same position would contribute if given the same percentage of team plate appearances. VORP does not consider the quality of a player's defense.

BABIP (batting average on balls in play) tells us how often a ball in play fell for a hit, and can help us identify whether a batter may have been lucky or not ... but note that high BABIPs also tend to follow the great hitters of our time, as well as speedy singles hitters who put the ball on the ground.

The next item is **BRR** (Baserunning Runs), which covers all of a player's baserunning accomplishments which includes (but isn't limited to) swiped bags and failed attempts. Next is **FRAA** (Fielding Runs Above Average), which also includes the number of games previously played at each position noted in parentheses. Multi-position players have only their two most frequent positions listed here, but their total FRAA number reflects all positions played.

Our last column here is **WARP** (Wins Above Replacement Player). WARP estimates the total value of a player, which means for hitters it takes into account hitting runs above average (calculated using the DRC+ model), BRR and FRAA. Then, it makes an adjustment for positions played and gives the player a credit for plate appearances based upon the difference between "replacement level"¬–which is derived from the quality of players added to a team's roster after the start of the season¬–and the league average.

Catchers

Catchers are a special breed, and thus they have earned their own separate box which displays some of the defensive metrics that we've built just for them. As an example, let's check out J.T. Realmuto.

YEAR	TEAM	P. COUNT	FRM RUNS	BLK RUNS	THRW RUNS	TOT RUNS
2016	MIA	18935	-8.5	1.8	2.1	-5.6
2017	MIA	18959	5.3	1.7	1.0	9.1
2018	MIA	16399	-0.4	0.9	0.1	0.4
2019	PHI	18448	-1.4	1.5	0.7	0.8

The **YEAR** and **TEAM** columns match what you'd find in the other stat box. **P. COUNT** indicates the number of pitches thrown while the catcher was behind the plate, including swinging strikes, fouls, and balls in play. **FRM RUNS** is the total run value the catcher provided (or cost) his team by influencing the umpire to call strikes where other catchers did not. **BLK RUNS** expresses the total run value above or below average for the catcher's ability to prevent wild pitches and passed balls. **THRW RUNS** is calculated using a similar model as the previous two statistics, and it measures a catcher's ability to throw out basestealers but also to dissuade them from testing his arm in the first place. It takes into account factors like the pitcher (including his delivery and pickoff move) and baserunner (who could be as fast as Billy Hamilton or as slow as Yonder Alonso). **TOT RUNS** is the sum of all of the previous three statistics.

Pitchers

Let's give our pitchers a turn, using 2018 NL Cy Young winner Jacob deGrom as our example. Take a look at his first stat block: the first line and the **YEAR**, **TEAM**, **LVL** and **AGE** columns are the same as in the position player example earlier.

Here too, we have a series of columns that display raw, unadjusted statistics compiled by the pitcher over the course of a season: **W** (wins), **L** (losses), **SV** (saves), **G** (games pitched), **GS** (games started), **IP** (innings pitched), **H** (hits allowed) and **HR** (home runs allowed). Next we have two statistics that are rates: **BB/9** (walks per nine innings) and **K/9** (strikeouts per nine innings), before returning to the unadjusted **K** (strikeouts).

Next up is **GB%** (ground ball percentage), which is the percentage of all batted balls that were hit in the ground, including both outs and hits. Remember, this is based on observational data and subject to human error, so please approach this with a healthy dose of skepticism.

BABIP (batting average on balls in play) is calculated using the same methodology as it is for position players, but it often tells us more about a pitcher than it does a hitter. With pitchers, a high BABIP is often due to poor defense or bad luck, and can often be an indicator of potential rebound, and a low BABIP may be cause to expect performance regression. (A typical league-average BABIP is close to .290-.300.)

After a witty 150ish words on the player like only Baseball Prospectus's staff can provide, it's on to that second stat block, which repeats the YEAR, TEAM, LVL, and AGE columns. The metrics **WHIP** (walks plus hits per inning pitched) and **ERA**

Texas Rangers 2019

(earned run average) are old standbys: WHIP measures walks and hits allowed on a per-inning basis, while ERA measures earned runs on a nine-inning basis. Neither of these stats are translated or adjusted.

DRA (Deserved Run Average) was described at length earlier, and measures how many runs the pitcher "deserved" to allow per nine innings. Please note that since we lack all the data points that would make for a "real" DRA for minor-league events, the DRA displayed for minor league partial-seasons is based off of different data. (That data is a modified version of our cFIP metric, which you can find more information about on our website.)

Jacob deGrom RHP
Born: 06/19/88   Age: 31   Bats: L   Throws: R
Height: 6'4"   Weight: 180   Origin: Round 9, 2010 Draft (#272 overall)

YEAR	TEAM	LVL	AGE	W	L	SV	G	GS	IP	H	HR	BB/9	K/9	K	GB%	BABIP
2016	NYN	MLB	28	7	8	0	24	24	148	142	15	2.2	8.7	143	47%	.312
2017	NYN	MLB	29	15	10	0	31	31	201^1	180	28	2.6	10.7	239	48%	.305
2018	NYN	MLB	30	10	9	0	32	32	217	152	10	1.9	11.2	269	48%	.281
2019	NYN	MLB	31	13	9	0	31	31	186	145	18	2.3	10.7	221	46%	.286

Breakout: 8%   Improve: 29%   Collapse: 28%   Attrition: 6%   MLB: 85%
Comparables: Erik Bedard, A.J. Burnett, CC Sabathia

YEAR	TEAM	LVL	AGE	WHIP	ERA	DRA	WARP	MPH	FB%	WHF	CSP
2016	NYN	MLB	28	1.20	3.04	3.30	3.5	96.3	59.6	12.1	47.2
2017	NYN	MLB	29	1.19	3.53	3.02	5.7	97.2	55.5	14.5	49.5
2018	NYN	MLB	30	0.91	1.70	2.09	8.0	98.2	52.1	16.3	48.4
2019	NYN	MLB	31	1.02	2.91	3.23	3.9	96.6	54.5	14.8	48.2

Just like with hitters, **WARP** (Wins Above Replacement Player) is a total value metric that puts pitchers of all stripes on the same scale as position players. We use DRA as the primary input for our calculation of WARP. You might notice that relief pitchers (due to their limited innings) may have a lower WARP than you were expecting or than you might see in other WARP-like metrics. WARP does not take leverage into account, just the actions a pitcher performs and the expected value of those actions … which ends up judging high-leverage relief pitchers differently than you might imagine given their prestige and market value.

MPH gives you the pitcher's 95th percentile velocity for the noted season, in order to give you an idea of what the *peak* fastball velocity a pitcher possesses. Since this comes from our pitch tracking data, it is not publicly available for minor-league pitchers.

Finally, we display the three new pitching metrics we described earlier. **FB%** (fastball percentage) gives you the percentage of fastballs thrown out of all pitches. **WhiffRt** (whiff rate) tells you the percentage of swinging strikes induced out of all pitches. **CS Prob** (called strike probability) expresses the likelihood of all pitches thrown to result in a called strike, after controlling for factors like handedness, umpire, pitch type, count, and location.

PECOTA

All players have PECOTA projections for 2019, as well as a set of other numbers that describe the performance of comparable players according to PECOTA. All projections for 2019 are for the player at the date we went to press in early January and are projected into the league and park context as indicated by the team abbreviation. All PECOTA projected statistics represent a player's projected major-league performance.

The numbers beneath the player's stats–Breakout, Improve, Collapse, Attrition–are part and parcel of the PECOTA projections. They estimate the likelihood of changes in performance relative to the player's previously-established level of production, based on the performance of comparable players:

Breakout Rate is the percent change that a player's production will improve by at least 20 percent relative to the weighted average of his performance over his most recent seasons.

Improve Rate is the percent chance that a player's production will improve at all relative to his baseline performance. A player who is expected to perform just the same as he has in the recent past will have an Improve Rate of 50 percent.

Collapse Rate is the percent chance that a position player's production will decline by at least 25 percent relative to his baseline performance.

Attrition Rate operates on playing time rather than performance. Specifically, it measures the likelihood that a player's playing time will decrease by at least 50 percent relative to his established level.

Breakout Rate and Collapse Rate can sometimes be counterintuitive for players who have already experienced a radical change in performance level. It's also worth noting that the projected decline in a player's rate performances might not be indicative of an expected decline in underlying ability or skill, but could just be an anticipated correction following a breakout season.

MLB% is the percentage of similar players who played in the major leagues in their relevant season.

The final pieces of information are the player's three highest-scoring comparable players as determined by PECOTA. All comparables represent a snapshot of how the listed player was performing at the same age as the current player, so if a 23-year-old pitcher is compared to Bartolo Colon, he's actually being compared to a 23-year-old Colon, not the version that pitched for the Rangers in 2018, nor to Colon's career as a whole.

Texas Rangers 2019

A few points about pitcher projections. First, we aren't yet projecting peak velocity, so that column will be blank in the PECOTA lines. Second, projecting DRA is trickier than evaluating past performance, because it is unclear how deserving each pitcher will be of his anticipated outcomes. However, we know that another DRA-related statistic–contextual FIP or cFIP–estimates future run scoring very well. So for PECOTA, the projected DRA figures you see are based on the past cFIPs generated by the pitcher and comparable players over time, along with the other factors described above.

Lineouts

In each chapter's Lineouts section, you'll find abbreviated text comments, as well as most of same information you'd find in our full player comments. We limit the stats boxes in this section to only including the 2018 information for each player.

Exclusive Player Visualizations

In our constant battle to provide you with new and interesting baseball content you can't find anywhere else, we've added a trio of data visualizations to each hitter's entry in these books and a pair of visualizations for each pitcher.

For hitters, you'll find three new infographics. The first is each player's **Batted Ball Distribution**, which displays the five major sections of the field: LF (left), LCF (left center), CF (center), RCF (right center), and RF (right). The percentage indicated tells us what percentage of batted balls from that hitter fell within that part of the field during the 2018 season. We've also included the hitter's slugging percentage on balls in play (also called **SLGCON**) for that part of the field.

You'll also see two heatmaps: **Strike Zone vs LHP** and **Strike Zone vs RHP**. These heat maps represent a view of the strike zone from behind the catcher. Areas where there is a darker coloration represent the places where a higher percentage of pitches resulted in hits. In other words, the heatmap represents a hitter's "sweet spots" for getting hits against either left-handed or right-handed pitchers, depending on the image.

Pitchers get two images that help explain what their pitches look like from a hitter's perspective: **Pitch Shape vs LHH** and **Pitch Shape vs RHH**. These images show you the shape and the "tunneling" effect of each pitcher's offerings from the batter's perspective. For each type of pitch that a pitcher throws (represented by an indicator shape), there's a set of dots indicating the flight path, where each dot represents a 0.01-second interval. This maps the average trajectory and speed of an offering, ending where the ball crosses the plate. The solid black box represents the regular strike zone, while the gray contour lines indicate the range of locations that a pitcher typically works in.

Below the image, we provide a bit more detailed information about each pitcher's average offering in the **Pitch Types** box. Here, we also list each of the pitcher's major offerings under the **Type** column.

- **Fastballs** (which usually refers to the four-seam variation)
- **Sinkers** and/or two-seam fastballs
- **Cutters** (which could include "hard" cutters like cut fastballs and "soft" cutters that resemble hard sliders)
- **Changeups** (not including most splitters)
- **Splitters** (split-fingered pitches, forkballs, and some split-changes)
- **Sliders** and/or slurves
- **Curveballs** (including spike-curveballs and knuckle-curveballs, as well as some slurvy curves)
- **Slow curveballs** and/or eephus pitches
- **Knuckleballs**
- **Screwballs**

The **Freq** column indicates the percentage of overall pitches that fall into each of those type categories; if a pitcher has a 16.55% score for changeups, then that's the percent of all pitches that he throws as changeups. **Velo** is exactly what you think it is: the average miles per hour for each pitch type. **H Mov** is the number of inches of horizontal movement on the average pitch of that type, while **V Mov** is the number of inches of vertical movement on the average pitch of that type. (At Baseball Prospectus, we measure this over the long flight of the ball and include gravity into the V Mov number in order to give you the most realistic representation of what the pitch *actually* does.)

If you're wondering about the second number in brackets, that's the index for that velocity or movement compared to the league average. Like DRC+, a score of 100 means that the speed or movement is about the same as league average, while a higher score means that there's higher velocity or movement than the league average. Numbers below 100 indicate less velocity or movement than the league average.

Part 1: Team Analysis

Table for Three: Previewing the 2019 Texas Rangers

Aaron Gleeman, Tim McCullough and Kate Morrison

Who will be the Rangers' breakout player for 2019?

KATE MORRISON: Let's say Shelby Miller, because someone has to. If he can stay healthy, maybe he can find the form that's eluded him for the last three seasons—and the Rangers could use a pitching surprise given how thin that rotation is.

AARON GLEEMAN: I realize the Willie Calhoun hype train failed to arrive as scheduled, but he's still only 24 years old and seems like the epitome of a post-hype sleeper. His first 100 plate appearances at age 23 were ugly, but that's common. His power was way down in Triple-A, which is worrisome for a player whose bat will have to carry him, but he also hit .294 with just 47 strikeouts in 470 plate appearances for Round Rock. I'm definitely lowering expectations compared to where they stood a year ago at this time, and it's not clear that there will even be a spot for him in the majors early on, but I'm still a believer and PECOTA sort of agrees, pegging Calhoun for a .440 slugging percentage.

TIM MCCULLOUGH: Well, after digging through the roster top to bottom, I can't put my finger on any single player with the pedigree to break out. Calhoun needs to figure out where his power went, so I'm not sure I can agree with PECOTA's outlook for him this season. If a "breakout" is going to come from anywhere, it appears it will have to be from the pitching staff. One of the "Tommy John trio" could find the fountain of youth and come back with renewed velocity. It will be a bit of a surprise to see them also feature good control so quickly, but it could happen. If I was forced to bet on one of them, Drew Smyly would be my choice. He's always had decent strikeout rates and seemed to do well at keeping the ball in the park when healthy. He's just 30 years old, so there's still a chance he has some bullets left in his arm.

Which Rangers player do you see collapsing in 2019?

AARON: I guess the obvious one here is Shin-Soo Choo, just because he's 36 years old, but he actually had a very solid 2018 after a decent 2017, and PECOTA projects him as an above-average hitter. Obviously given his lack of defensive value and his salary that makes him a marginal all-around player, but with two years (and $42 million) left on his contract, what are the odds he remains with the Rangers? A repeat of last season (.264/.377/.434) could help quite a few teams. It can help the Rangers too, but if things go downhill early what happens with Choo?

TIM: It looks to me like the Rangers are at least somewhat concerned about Choo as their fourth outfielder. If you assume they're starting Mazara, Gallo, and DeShields then the only real spots open are at DH and fourth outfielder. They must lack faith in Carlos Tocci, Willie Calhoun, and possibly even Choo since they went out and signed Hunter Pence and Ben Revere, albeit to minor league deals. I just can't figure what their thinking is. Calhoun has nothing left to prove in the minors. If they're ever going to give him a shot to learn at the Major League level, one would think this is the year to do it. Choo is as steady a player as you're going to find but he did fade badly over the second half last year. I wouldn't be surprised if he was entering his decline phase.

KATE: It's hard to pick someone to collapse off this roster because it seems like most players are either pretty solid (Elvis Andrus), likely to be solidly in-line with their projections (Rougned Odor, Delino DeShields, half the pitching staff), or hopeful pleasant surprises (Ronald Guzman, Nomar Mazara, the other half of the pitching staff).

What part of the Rangers can you simply not go along with PECOTA?

KATE: I mean, I'm *deeply* disappointed that PECOTA is now projecting 70 wins rather than 69.

AARON: Rob McQuown has rejected hundreds of Trello tickets from me requesting that we round up/down everything from 60-68 wins and 70-78 wins to 69. It's his one negative trait. (Also: I've got to think Nomar Mazara takes at least a small step forward at some point.)

KATE: I agree on Mazara, having watched him in the minors. The talent is there and while he's not the flashiest of players, this could be the year he puts everything together. I'd at least think he hits more home runs than the 19 currently projected.

TIM: Mazara was in the process of taking that step forward last season by improving his hitting against left-handed pitchers. He had a .425 SLG vs. southpaws at the All-Star break, then he injured his thumb and his production tumbled across the board. He's penciled in as their cleanup hitter this season, so the opportunity to put up a big season will be there.

How will the Rangers end up, and what kind of path will they take to get there?

KATE: I think it's probable that they're at the bottom of the division, again. For the two or three exciting names on this team, there's quite a bit of mediocrity. There could be a break-out pitcher or two, and with a few tweaks they could pretend at contention, but right now, this is a team in stagnation. They could be an 80 win team if everything goes perfectly well, but they're more likely to limp to 67 wins and rely on that ballpark-closing concert by Billy Joel to make up the difference.

TIM: The scary thing about this team is their proposed starting rotation and the lack of depth behind it. Three of their current projected five starters are returning from Tommy John surgery—Edinson Volquez, Drew Smyly and Shelby Miller are all in camp and throwing but are they really going to be ready by April? After them on the depth chart: Yohander Mendez, Ariel Jurado, Joe Palumbo, Brock Burke and Taylor Hearn don't exactly inspire confidence if any of the trio of Tommy John returnees is delayed or gets injured again.

I have to believe that Jon Daniels is looking at the free agent pitchers that will be available next winter and is biding his time until then. Jake Arrieta, Stephen Strasburg, Gerrit Cole, Chris Archer, and Corey Kluber are all set to be on the market. Barring some sort of divine intervention, the Rangers won't contend this year, so signing a few reclamation projects who could bounce back seems totally rational. Of course, the fans won't look at it that way.

AARON: I like their overall lineup better than I expected to, but yeah, the pitching is pretty bad and has a chance to look really bad by midseason. Might this be a team with no real middle-ground scenario—they either win 78 games, holding things together enough to surprise some people, or injuries and trades lead to a stripped-down roster on the way to 65 wins?

How did the Rangers approach the offseason, and did they do well, given their aims?

AARON: They clearly wanted to bring in some veterans to help keep things afloat while they sift through potential long-term building blocks all season. I liked a lot of their short-term pickups quite a bit, on a low-wattage scale. Drew Smyly, Asdrubal Cabrera, Shawn Kelley, Jesse Chavez, Shelby Miller—I think all of those guys have a chance to provide good value for minimal risk, and maybe a couple can be spun off for prospects in July. Giving a three-year, $30 million deal to Lance Lynn confused the hell out of me, especially relative to those other deals, although I'm willing to admit that watching Lynn for 20 starts in Minnesota last year ruined my ability to see him as anything but someone to avoid.

TIM: Looking over the roster, I think trading was clearly part of their signing strategy this winter, especially their bullpen. If any of their bullpen squad puts together a decent first half, look for Daniels to take advantage of the dearth of arms available and trade them away for whatever pieces for the future he can get. Same goes for their starters. If Volquez, Smyly, or Miller can piece together a good half, they'll go too. When you consider that most of the Rangers' better arms in the minors are in the lower levels, their signings and strategy make sense. However, I have to agree that signing Lynn for three years is a true head scratcher. His control was non-existent last year (not that it was ever great) and he was hit hard, especially his fastball. Not one of his pitches produced positive value last season, and his 35.4% Hard% last year was well above his 29.7% career mark.

KATE: The Lynn deal is confusing but maybe they think that with a new pitching coach and a new environment they can squeeze either those three years out or trade him at the deadline. They clearly had a directive to do the most with very little and you could argue that they've accomplished it—but what's the purpose of having very little? There's not much in the farm system coming to save them. The division isn't a weak one. They could have spent on the solid free agents out there, and decided not to.

How do the Rangers approach winning differently from other teams, and how does it shape their identity?

KATE: For whatever it's worth, the Rangers have yet to engage in a full-on teardown. Sure, they've gotten worse by pieces over the last few years, but they've at least attempted to field a team, and even now, at their most mediocre, they're really only a few pieces and a few prospects away from being something really special again. Will it work? Probably not this season.

As for the identity part, I could go on for hours on the Rangers' identity but no one's here for that.

AARON: Maybe it's just because of the team at the top of the division, and how they got there, but with more and more teams going into full-on rebuild/teardown mode, the few teams that choose the less extreme path are interesting to me. Texas is one, like you said. I think baseball would be better off if "rebuilding" didn't necessarily mean stripping the entire team for parts and being horrible for five years, but by not doing that are the Rangers setting themselves up for a long-term home in the middle?

TIM: I'm having a tough time finding any real identity here. It seems like they want to be a "home run powerhouse" team but they don't really have the personnel on the roster to do it. They certainly aren't going to manufacture runs with a team OBP of .318 and just 74 stolen bases. They had the fifth-most runners left on base in the AL, so a little clutch hitting would go a long way. They'd do really well to add a couple of high-contact hitters who can run a bit.

What is your prediction for the Rangers' season record?

AARON: I'll be slightly more optimistic than PECOTA and say 74-88, which might actually be good (or not bad) enough to avoid last place in the AL West.

KATE: Roster as it is—in that 70-75 win range.

TIM: I'll go with 72-90 and watch the dog race between the Rangers and Mariners for last place.

Performance Graphs

2018 Hit List Ranking

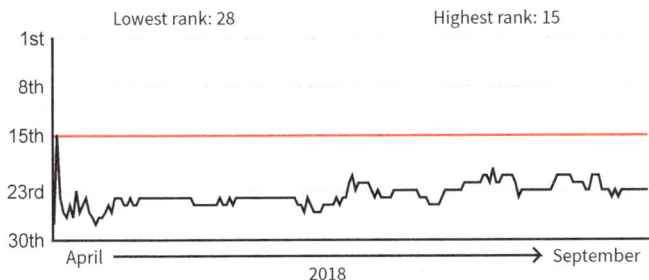

Committed Payroll (in millions)

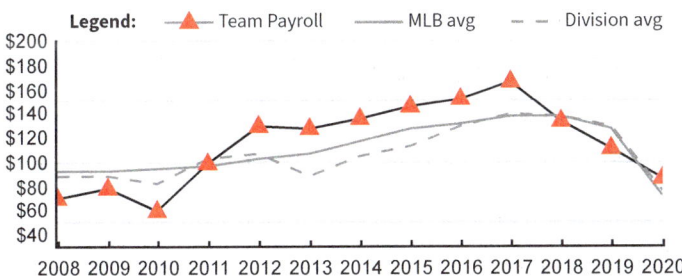

Farm System Ranking

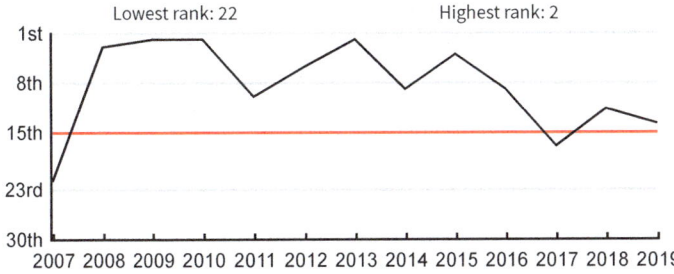

2018 Team Performance

ACTUAL STANDINGS

Team	W	L	Pct
HOU	103	59	.635
OAK	97	65	.598
SEA	89	73	.549
ANA	80	82	.493
TEX	**67**	**95**	**.413**

THIRD-ORDER STANDINGS

Team	W	L	Pct
HOU	108	54	.666
OAK	96	66	.592
SEA	82	80	.506
ANA	80	82	.493
TEX	**68**	**94**	**.419**

TOP HITTERS

Player	WARP
Joey Gallo	2.7
Rougned Odor	2.4
Shin-Soo Choo	2.2

TOP PITCHERS

Player	WARP
Cole Hamels	1.6
Jose Leclerc	1.4
Jesse Chavez	0.9

VITAL STATISTICS

Statistic Name	Value	Rank
Pythagenpat	.433	21st
Runs Scored per Game	4.55	14th
Runs Allowed per Game	5.23	28th
Deserved Runs Created Plus	97	15th
Deserved Run Average	5.99	30th
Fielding Independent Pitching	4.82	29th
Defensive Efficiency Rating	.701	21st
Batter Age	27.5	10th
Pitcher Age	31.0	30th
Salary	$133.1M	16th
Marginal $ per Marginal Win	$6.5M	5th
Disabled List Days	$1,600.0M	28th
$ on DL	14%	11th

2019 Team Projections

PROJECTED STANDINGS

Team	W	L	Pct	+/-
HOU	98	64	.604	-5
ANA	80	82	.493	0
OAK	79	83	.487	-18
TEX	**71**	**91**	**.438**	**+4**
SEA	70	92	.432	-19

TOP PROJECTED HITTERS

Player	WARP
Elvis Andrus	2.7
Joey Gallo	2.1
Jeff Mathis	2.0

TOP PROJECTED PITCHERS

Player	WARP
Lance Lynn	1.6
Shelby Miller	1.4
Jonathan Hernandez	0.9

FARM SYSTEM REPORT

Top Prospect	Number of Top 101 Prospects
Leody Taveras, #47	4

KEY DEDUCTIONS

Player	WARP
Jurickson Profar	2.4
Robinson Chirinos	0.6
Martin Perez	0.6
Drew Robinson	0.4
Matt Moore	0.3
Alex Claudio	0.3

KEY ADDITIONS

Player	WARP
Jeff Mathis	2.0
Lance Lynn	1.6
Shelby Miller	1.4
Asdrubal Cabrera	0.6
Logan Forsythe	0.5
Taylor Guerrieri	0.4

Team Personnel

President, General Manager
Jon Daniels

Manager
Chris Woodward

BP Alumni
Bradley Ankrom
Andrew Koo
Amy Pircher

Globe Life Park in Arlington Stats

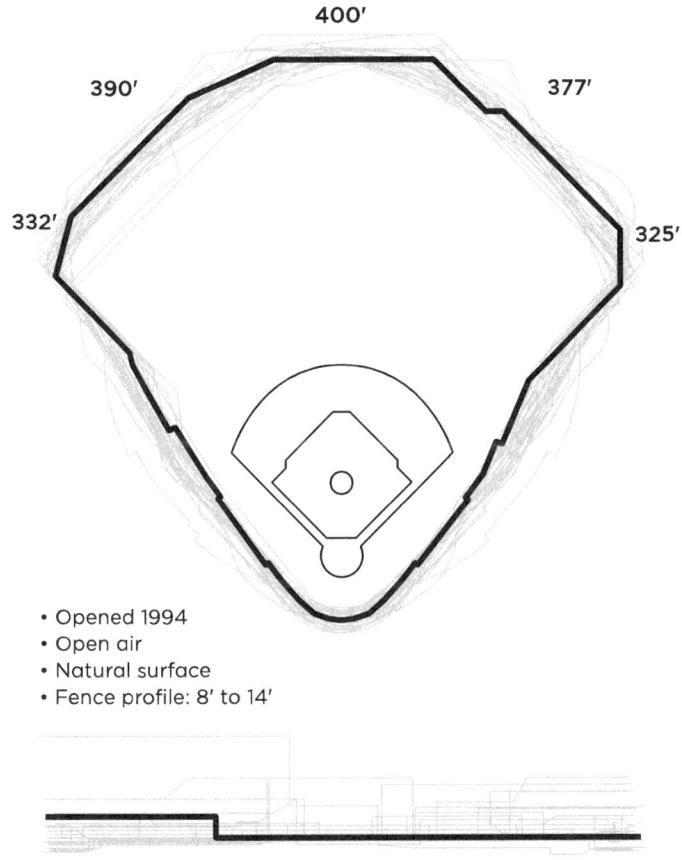

- Opened 1994
- Open air
- Natural surface
- Fence profile: 8' to 14'

Three-Year Park Factors

Runs	Runs/RH	Runs/LH	HR/RH	HR/LH
108	108	108	104	107

Rangers Team Analysis

Baseball has experienced an influx of knowledge over the past 15 years. The value of on-base percentage was discovered and re-discovered, fielders realized they'd often been standing in the wrong place the last hundred-odd years, catchers are being signed specifically because they can frame well and the metrics once limited to the pages of "Baseball Prospectus" have appeared frequently on MLB Network. And yet despite all of that innovation, we're still no closer to understanding how pitchers work.

It doesn't matter whether they receive a normal workload or whether they get wrapped in bubble wrap, pitchers remain unpredictable. They get hurt. Their stuff backs up. Their killer changeup that worked in rookie ball suddenly twists straight at bats as they move up the ladder. Pitchers exist to break your heart, and the Rangers have suffered a lot of heartbreak over the years.

The pitcher most synonymous with the franchise is Nolan Ryan, who only played for the team for five seasons, and whose freakish durability remains the stuff of legend. Ryan may not have been the best pitcher in history, but he might have been the most consistent pitcher in history. He showed up every start, always seemed to have the same stuff, year after year. But Ryan wasn't drafted or developed by the Rangers. He came to the team a finished product.

That's been a common refrain for the organization throughout its history. Many of the best pitchers to suit up for the Rangers established themselves elsewhere and were either signed as free agents or brought in via trades. In the 47 years they've existed, the Rangers have failed to draft and develop a bonafide ace.

Sure, the team has had a few successes. Kenny Rogers and Kevin Brown both put up solid numbers, though accumulated much of their value away from the team. Derek Holland was OK. Colby Lewis needed a stint in Japan, but he eventually produced. Edinson Volquez had some decent seasons after being traded away. Those players represent some of the team's biggest pitching wins. The losses have been far more numerous and—sorry, Rangers fans—include players like Kevin Mathews, Chad Hawkins, Corey Lee, Eric Hurley, Thomas Diamond, Blake Beavan…the list goes on and on and on some more.

It's not for lack of trying. The team has tried various approaches to finding its first home-grown ace. They tried the aggressive straight-to-the-majors method with David Clyde, then watched him fall apart before he could buy alcohol. They tried the break-em-in-as-a-reliever method with Neftali Feliz. They drafted 24 pitchers in the first or supplemental round in the past 18 years in hopes that throwing more pitchers at the problem might solve it. They even tried to bring Ryan back as team president so he could get pitchers on his old throwing program. None of those strategies worked.

Now, the Rangers are fully ensconced in a multiyear rebuild; the veterans have been distributed to other teams or been handed severance packages, and the rotation is stocked with injury-riddled bounce-back candidates like Mike Minor and Drew Smyly, auditioning for deadline deals to contenders. Few of the pitchers on this roster will see the next good Rangers team. In an attempt to buck their historical struggles and finally develop a couple top-line starters—or perhaps out of desperation—the Rangers are trying an inventive and controversial new pitching strategy. The team is attempting to develop pitching prospects by not having them throw a single pitch.

Before you panic and declare the Rangers everything wrong with baseball today, understand it isn't as drastic as it sounds. Over the past three years, the Rangers have selected certain high school draftees as candidates for something they call their de-load program.

The de-load program gives young pitchers in the organization an opportunity to learn every aspect of pitching without having them take the mound in games until the following June, according to the team's director of minor-league operations Paul Kruger. "We really wanted to spend as much time as we could educating them on baseball, injury prevention, growing their bodies naturally…while also learning the values of having a good throwing program," he says. "It was like a truly comprehensive orientation to professional baseball and pitching as a professional." Kruger, who has been with the team since 2009, was one of the main proponents of the idea. He was joined by pitching coordinator Danny Clark, who has been with the club for 14 years.

They helped launch the program in 2016, though some changes have been made since then. Initially, pitchers were allowed to throw a few innings before the end of the year. Last season was the first year the pitchers in the de-load program did not throw a single pitch in a game the year they were drafted. Despite those changes, one thing has always remained consistent. The program is just for a handful of high school draftees. Only five pitchers went through the de-load program in 2018.

There are reasons the team only puts high school pitchers through the program. The human body is still developing quite a bit between 18 and 22, according to Kruger, and there's no reason to push those players considering how much they threw prior to getting drafted. Another part of it deals with the extreme life changes that come with entering professional baseball straight out of high school.

"You are going from a small town where you are really the star—you're the show," Kruger says. "To a professional on your own, staying at a hotel, having to cook your own meals and you're getting a paycheck, just balancing all these different things. Oh wait, and you have to play baseball?"

Mostly, though, it just made sense to Clark and Kruger. To them, the transition from high school to pro ball should be just like any other job. "You go into any job and you get trained," Clark says. "And then you do the job. And I just feel like that was one of the things I always thought about: Educating our players in all aspects before we allow them to go and compete."

None of this comes as a surprise to the players selected to take part in the de-load program. The team meets with each player and their families to talk about the decision. During those meetings, the team lays out a complete calendar from the day the pitcher was drafted through June of the following year. The Rangers make sure everyone involved is on board with the idea before a pitcher joined the program.

Even though the players know what they're getting into, there's still an urge to compete, especially when they see other players take the mound. But the players who have gone through the program have said nothing but good things about it. "When they first hear about it, it's kinda like 'what,'" Clark says. "Then they get into it. When they come out of it, I've heard nothing but raves about it."

Players who have not gone through the program have expressed regret that they weren't able to do it, according to Kruger. But that doesn't mean the de-load program has been a complete success. The group of players who have gone through it—which includes Alex Speas, Cole Ragans, Scott Engler, Tyree Thompson, Tai Tiedemann, Hans Crouse, Seth Nordlin, Cole Winn, Owen White, Destin Dotson, among others—has experienced varying degrees of struggle in the brief time they've taken the mound. Despite the team carefully monitoring workload, both Speas and Ragans needed to undergo Tommy John surgery. Clark was hesitant to say their reduced usage led to the injuries, but couldn't fully rule it out either.

"Did that contribute, who knows? I would hate to say that slowing the process had to do with what injury came into play," he says.

Given the players involved in the de-load program, it's going to be years before anyone knows whether it's paying off. High school players generally need at least a few seasons before they reach the majors. Once they get there, it could take a couple more before they're considered finished products. Drawing conclusions on any of these players five years after they are drafted might be too soon, and five years is a long time in baseball. Coaching staffs and front offices have been cleaned out and turned over in shorter amounts of time. Even if those pitchers fail, it might not be a result of the de-load program. It could easily be a case of pitchers being pitchers.

So why do it?

Sticking with the status quo hasn't led to success for the Rangers. After trying to develop pitchers every other way, the team decided a drastic departure from the norm was worth a shot.

The Rangers don't need the de-load program to solve the pitcher, they just need it to help. While an army of aces would be nice, one top-line starter and a few mid-rotation assets would be a massive upgrade over what the team has experienced lately. This season will be crucial in determining whether that's going to happen. While the pitchers in the de-load program likely won't pitch in the majors in 2019, their health and development will give the team a window into whether the counterintuitive process will be talked about as a major breakthrough within the game 15 years from now.

Until then, the Rangers have brought back Volquez to eat some innings until the students of the de-load program are ready to graduate to the majors. Because innovation and desperation are a lot closer than anyone is willing to admit.

—Chris Cwik is a writer at Yahoo! Sports.

Part 2: Player Analysis

Elvis Andrus SS

Born: 08/26/88   Age: 30   Bats: R   Throws: R
Height: 6'0"   Weight: 200   Origin: International Free Agent, 2005

YEAR	TEAM	LVL	AGE	PA	R	2B	3B	HR	RBI	BB	K	SB	CS	AVG/OBP/SLG
2016	TEX	MLB	27	568	75	31	7	8	69	47	70	24	8	.302/.362/.439
2017	TEX	MLB	28	689	100	44	4	20	88	38	101	25	10	.297/.337/.471
2018	TEX	MLB	29	428	53	20	3	6	33	28	66	5	3	.256/.308/.367
2019	TEX	MLB	30	607	72	33	5	14	68	45	91	18	7	.282/.340/.437

Breakout: 2%   Improve: 40%   Collapse: 11%   Attrition: 15%   MLB: 100%
Comparables: Oscar Robles, Erick Aybar, Jack Wilson

Andrus entered 2018 as one of the storylines to keep an eye on: If he had a third consecutive season of improvement as part of his elite-offensive-shortstop renaissance, he might be more likely to opt out of his contract after the season and explore free agency. Instead, a Keynan Middleton fastball broke a bone in his right elbow and even after his return it took him awhile to get back in the groove at the plate. He chose to remain in Texas, with four years and $58 million left on his deal. However, he has another opt-out after the 2019 season, so let's hit the snooze button on that question and come back to it in a year.

YEAR	TEAM	LVL	AGE	PA	DRC+	VORP	BABIP	BRR	FRAA	WARP
2016	TEX	MLB	27	568	113	34.6	.333	1.4	SS(147): -4.1	3.2
2017	TEX	MLB	28	689	108	37.8	.325	2.8	SS(157): 16.2	5.7
2018	TEX	MLB	29	428	91	9.4	.292	0.5	SS(97): -6.4	0.8
2019	TEX	MLB	30	607	105	29.3	.311	0.8	SS -1	2.7

Elvis Andrus, continued

Batted Ball Distribution

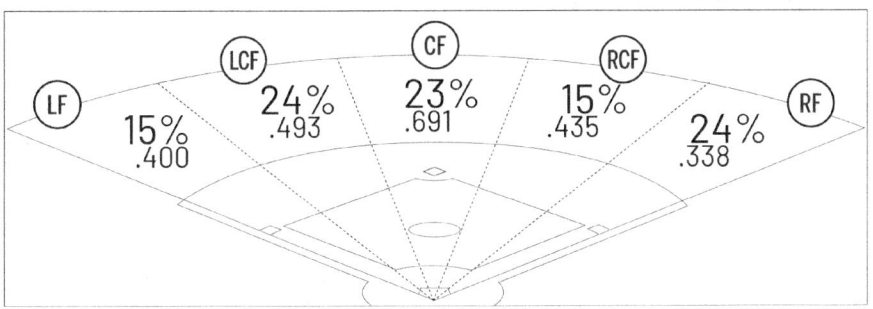

Strike Zone vs LHP

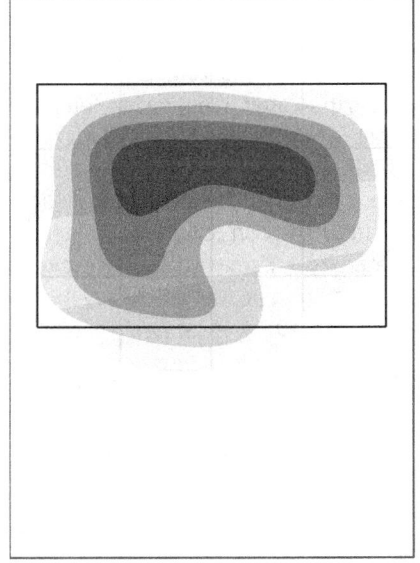

Strike Zone vs RHP

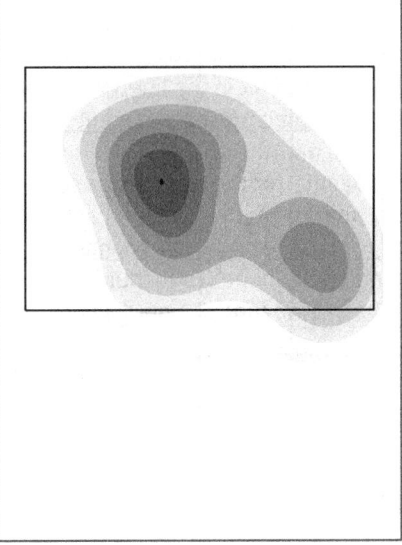

Asdrubal Cabrera INF

Born: 11/13/85 Age: 33 Bats: B Throws: R
Height: 6'0" Weight: 205 Origin: International Free Agent, 2002

YEAR	TEAM	LVL	AGE	PA	R	2B	3B	HR	RBI	BB	K	SB	CS	AVG/OBP/SLG
2016	NYN	MLB	30	568	65	30	1	23	62	38	103	5	1	.280/.336/.474
2017	NYN	MLB	31	540	66	32	0	14	59	50	83	3	2	.280/.351/.434
2018	NYN	MLB	32	407	48	23	1	18	58	29	81	0	0	.277/.329/.488
2018	PHI	MLB	32	185	20	13	0	5	17	12	38	0	0	.228/.286/.392
2019	TEX	MLB	33	474	60	26	2	14	52	36	86	2	1	.272/.333/.440

Breakout: 3% Improve: 32% Collapse: 8% Attrition: 7% MLB: 96%
Comparables: Aaron Hill, Brandon Phillips, Orlando Hudson

Picking up Cabrera was a less-than-tacit admission by the Phillies' front office that starting shortstop Scott Kingery was no longer tolerable for 2018. The messaging was unavoidable. At least, if it had been Manny Machado, the upgrade could've been justified with a sentence as simple as "because it's Manny Machado." Asdrubal Cabrera, though? That one's different. Cabrera was imported because he stood to provide an offensive upgrade for a team stuck eternally making left turns in a whirlpool, inching closer to the trough by the game. His poor defense at shortstop would be palatable, so long as he provided the expected lift in the lineup his Mets numbers indicated. Well, he too fell into the black pit of despair that entombed the rest of the Phillies offense over the last two months, with the traditional Asdrubalian defense intact. Cabrera enters free agency for the third time as a 33-year-old infielder without a clear position but, apart from being a bit of a drag for the Phils, has been reliable with the bat for some time now. He's probably best tolerated by a team with a good glove to bring off the bench, but could probably be expected to post a SLG-heavy high-.700s OPS no matter where he ends up playing in 2019.

YEAR	TEAM	LVL	AGE	PA	DRC+	VORP	BABIP	BRR	FRAA	WARP
2016	NYN	MLB	30	568	113	45.7	.310	0.1	SS(135): -4.2	3.0
2017	NYN	MLB	31	540	104	31.1	.310	-2.2	SS(45): -0.2, 3B(44): -1.1	1.8
2018	NYN	MLB	32	407	105	28.9	.309	1.9	2B(90): -10.8	0.6
2018	PHI	MLB	32	185	107	4.2	.266	0.5	SS(31): -0.6, 3B(22): -0.5	0.8
2019	TEX	MLB	33	474	104	14.7	.309	-0.7	3B -6, 2B -1	0.7

Asdrubal Cabrera, continued

Batted Ball Distribution

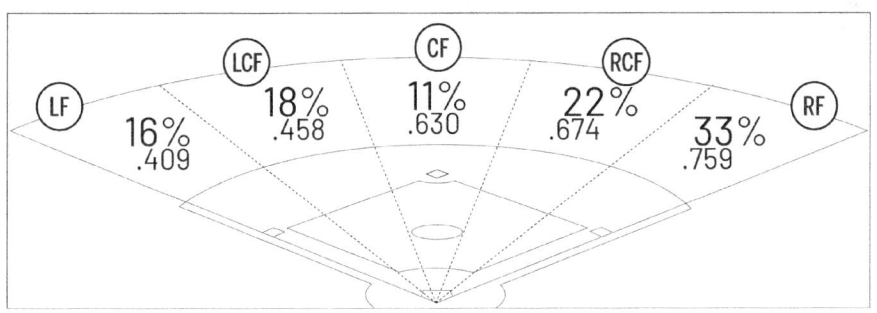

| **Strike Zone vs LHP** | **Strike Zone vs RHP** |

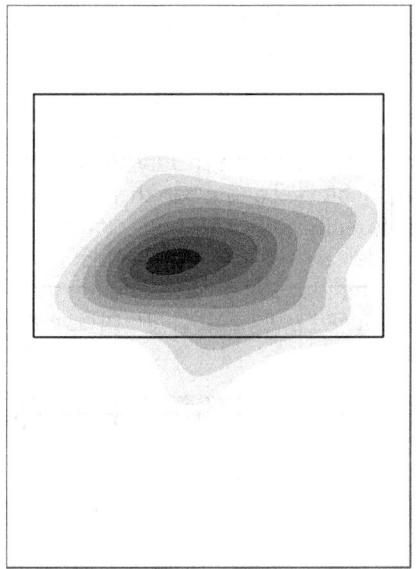
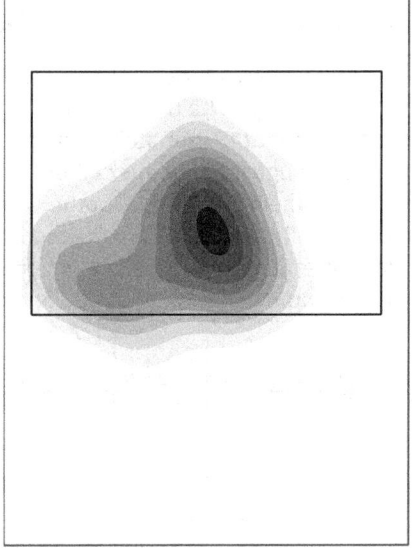

Willie Calhoun LF

Born: 11/04/94   Age: 24   Bats: L   Throws: R
Height: 5'8"   Weight: 187   Origin: Round 4, 2015 Draft (#132 overall)

YEAR	TEAM	LVL	AGE	PA	R	2B	3B	HR	RBI	BB	K	SB	CS	AVG/OBP/SLG
2016	TUL	AA	21	560	75	25	1	27	88	45	65	0	0	.254/.318/.469
2017	OKL	AAA	22	414	64	24	5	23	67	36	49	3	2	.298/.357/.574
2017	ROU	AAA	22	120	16	3	1	8	26	6	12	1	0	.310/.345/.566
2017	TEX	MLB	22	37	3	0	0	1	4	2	7	0	0	.265/.324/.353
2018	ROU	AAA	23	470	66	32	0	9	47	32	47	4	0	.294/.351/.431
2018	TEX	MLB	23	108	8	5	0	2	11	6	24	0	0	.222/.269/.333
2019	TEX	MLB	24	286	33	14	1	11	36	18	43	1	0	.243/.295/.430

Breakout: 13%   Improve: 41%   Collapse: 8%   Attrition: 27%   MLB: 68%
Comparables: Ramon Flores, J.D. Martinez, Jordan Luplow

After years of wondering if Calhoun could be something other than what he is, it's becoming evident that he's really just more of a Willie Calhoun type, which is to say: He's going to mash and he's going to play defense that causes you to reflexively make a sound that goes from low to high like a slide whistle. (But a few octaves lower. Go on, try it. You'll recognize it. OOOOOOooo^{ooo}•••...)

Calhoun was disappointed to start the season in Triple-A, and his stats showed it. In April, he hit .229 with a .673 OPS. But he improved in each successive month, ultimately hitting .429 with an 1.139 OPS in July. He tapered off a bit in August before his call-up, and again hit well enough in the big leagues to suggest the bat is ready, but the defense is really nothing to write home about. Ideally, you could plug Calhoun in at designated hitter and just let him go wild. But — at least at time of this writing — Shin-Soo Choo is still a Ranger, so while the prairie sky may be wide and high *CLAP CLAP CLAP CLAP* DH is full in Texas.

YEAR	TEAM	LVL	AGE	PA	DRC+	VORP	BABIP	BRR	FRAA	WARP
2016	TUL	AA	21	560	122	26.2	.242	0.3	2B(119): -9.8	0.6
2017	OKL	AAA	22	414	130	30.5	.289	-1.8	2B(74): 0.9, LF(12): -1.9	1.8
2017	ROU	AAA	22	120	130	10.0	.290	-1.2	LF(24): 2.4, 2B(3): -0.7	0.6
2017	TEX	MLB	22	37	87	1.1	.308	0.3	LF(11): -0.7	0.0
2018	ROU	AAA	23	470	119	14.3	.314	-3.2	LF(91): -11.9	0.0
2018	TEX	MLB	23	108	87	-2.5	.267	-0.7	LF(27): -2.8	-0.3
2019	TEX	MLB	24	286	89	2.4	.250	-0.4	LF -2	0.0

Willie Calhoun, continued

Batted Ball Distribution

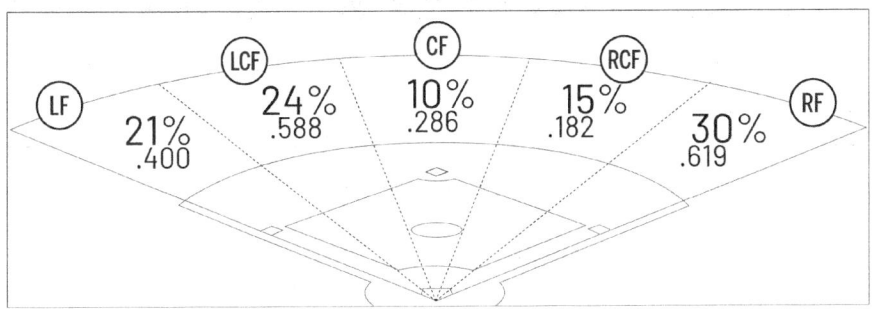

Strike Zone vs LHP

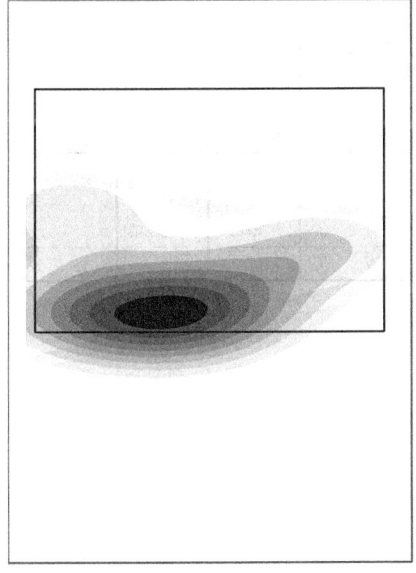

Strike Zone vs RHP

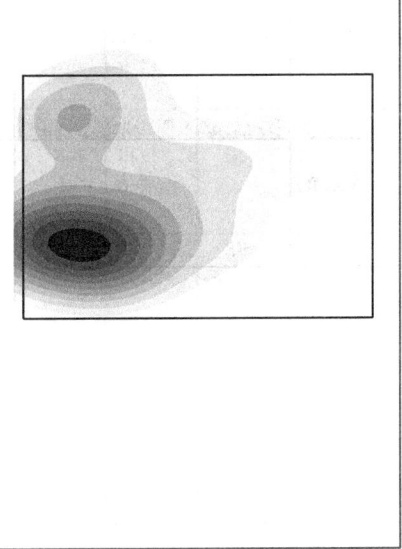

Shin-Soo Choo OF

Born: 07/13/82 Age: 36 Bats: L Throws: L
Height: 5'11" Weight: 210 Origin: International Free Agent, 2000

YEAR	TEAM	LVL	AGE	PA	R	2B	3B	HR	RBI	BB	K	SB	CS	AVG/OBP/SLG
2016	TEX	MLB	33	210	27	7	0	7	17	25	46	6	3	.242/.357/.399
2017	TEX	MLB	34	636	96	20	1	22	78	77	134	12	3	.261/.357/.423
2018	TEX	MLB	35	665	83	30	1	21	62	92	156	6	1	.264/.377/.434
2019	TEX	MLB	36	487	65	21	2	14	51	54	109	6	2	.256/.348/.415

Breakout: 0% Improve: 21% Collapse: 22% Attrition: 20% MLB: 80%
Comparables: Lyle Overbay, John Wockenfuss, Ryan Klesko

Choo had one of his best seasons in 2018, appearing in his first All-Star game at age 35 and stringing together a 52-game on-base streak. Will the continued productivity — combined with the fact that he has only two years left on what was once a behemoth contract — mean the Rangers will eat a glutton-sized serving of salary and make him the latest casualty of the three-year Arlington Purge? Probably not as a standalone equation, but once you factor in the Rangers' dearth of pitching and surfeit of left-handed corner bats, it all starts to add up. Or maybe "subtract" is the better math term to use here. I don't know, man; it's a big book and there are a lot of these to write.

YEAR	TEAM	LVL	AGE	PA	DRC+	VORP	BABIP	BRR	FRAA	WARP
2016	TEX	MLB	33	210	108	5.8	.288	-0.6	RF(43): -0.4	0.5
2017	TEX	MLB	34	636	105	11.1	.305	0.7	RF(77): -1.5	1.5
2018	TEX	MLB	35	665	116	25.7	.330	-0.9	RF(34): -2.0, LF(26): -0.6	2.2
2019	TEX	MLB	36	487	105	12.1	.310	-0.1	RF 0, LF 0	1.2

Shin-Soo Choo, continued

Batted Ball Distribution

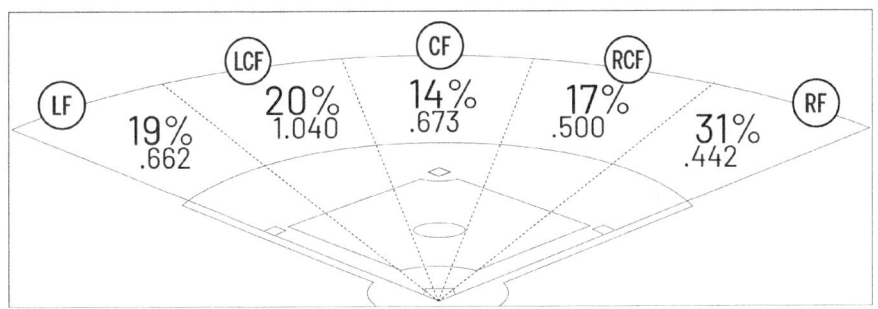

Strike Zone vs LHP **Strike Zone vs RHP**

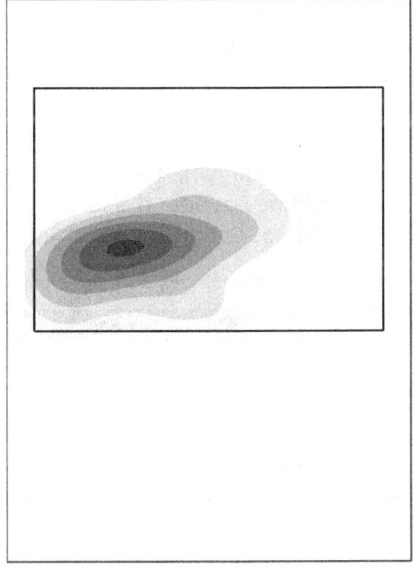
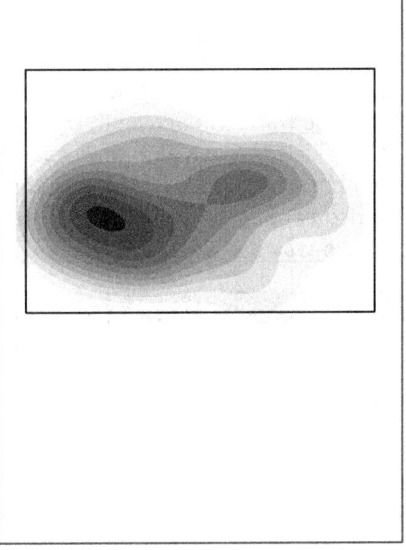

Matt Davidson   DH

Born: 03/26/91   Age: 28   Bats: R   Throws: R
Height: 6'3"   Weight: 230   Origin: Round 1, 2009 Draft (#35 overall)

YEAR	TEAM	LVL	AGE	PA	R	2B	3B	HR	RBI	BB	K	SB	CS	AVG/OBP/SLG
2016	CHR	AAA	25	326	35	20	0	10	46	32	86	0	0	.268/.349/.444
2016	CHA	MLB	25	2	1	0	0	0	1	0	1	0	0	.500/.500/.500
2017	CHA	MLB	26	443	43	16	1	26	68	19	165	0	1	.220/.260/.452
2018	CHA	MLB	27	496	51	23	0	20	62	52	165	0	0	.228/.319/.419
2019	TEX	MLB	28	70	8	3	0	3	9	6	21	0	0	.222/.300/.413

Breakout: 7%   Improve: 46%   Collapse: 16%   Attrition: 18%   MLB: 93%
Comparables: Jonny Gomes, Carlos Pena, Mark Trumbo

When Earth is a microwaved wasteland sometime in the next 12-to-112 years, will historians/masochists seeking to understand our time focus more on Davidson completely revamping his plate approach to transform himself into a decent hitter, or the three scoreless innings he threw to spell a bad pitching staff for a team that lost 100 games? Strangely enough, probably the latter. The modern bullpen features few right-handers who sit 90-91 mph with a looping splitter-like thing, but if Davidson winds up ushering in a wave of part-time position players who earn their keep by contributing non-embarrassing innings, his place in history will be secure. Less secure is his positional role, since his third base work is increasingly occasional. A late-season slide and a struggle to reclaim his approach after back spasms left him with a campaign that will make a first base gig hard to hold. Non-tendered by the White Sox after the season, Davidson appears to be betting on being part of the wave of the future, training as a two-way player.

YEAR	TEAM	LVL	AGE	PA	DRC+	VORP	BABIP	BRR	FRAA	WARP
2016	CHR	AAA	25	326	123	10.7	.346	-2.6	3B(66): 6.7, 1B(6): 0.1	1.8
2016	CHA	MLB	25	2	84	0.1	1.000	-0.1		0.0
2017	CHA	MLB	26	443	87	-7.8	.285	-3.4	3B(34): -1.9, 1B(19): -1.2	-0.4
2018	CHA	MLB	27	496	101	3.7	.313	-3.9	1B(45): -3.1, 3B(14): 0.9	0.3
2019	TEX	MLB	28	70	90	0.1	.306	-0.1	1B -1	-0.1

Matt Davidson, continued

Batted Ball Distribution

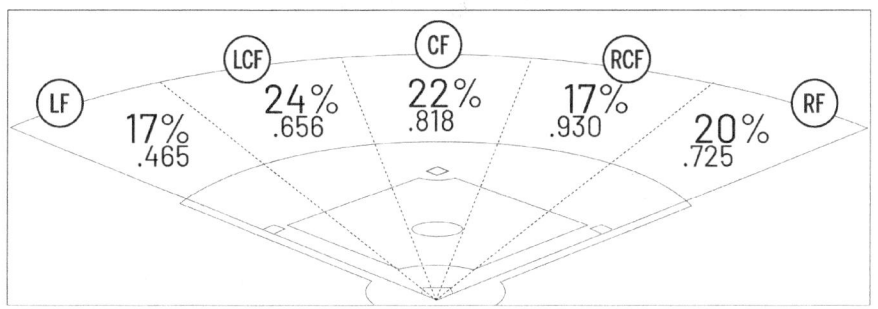

Strike Zone vs LHP

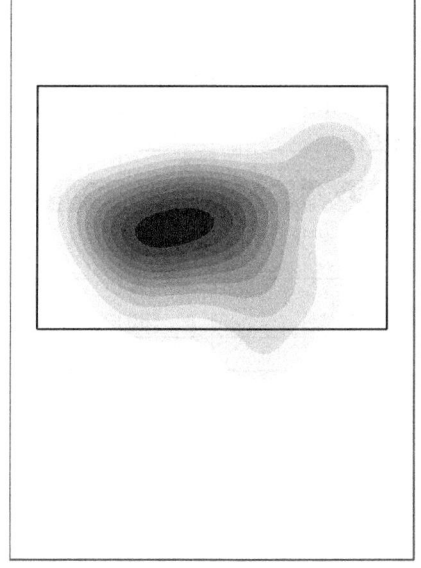

Strike Zone vs RHP

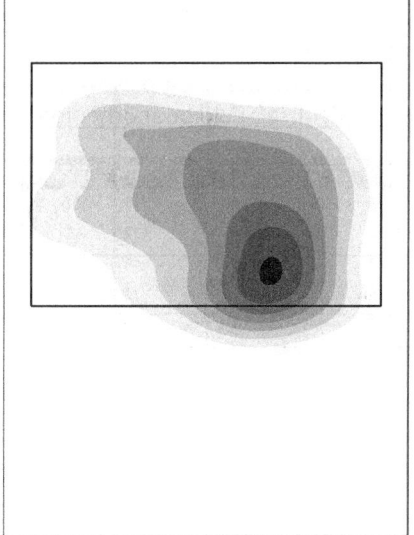

Delino DeShields CF
Born: 08/16/92 Age: 26 Bats: R Throws: R
Height: 5'9" Weight: 200 Origin: Round 1, 2010 Draft (#8 overall)

YEAR	TEAM	LVL	AGE	PA	R	2B	3B	HR	RBI	BB	K	SB	CS	AVG/OBP/SLG
2016	ROU	AAA	23	249	37	10	0	3	17	35	60	21	7	.261/.367/.353
2016	TEX	MLB	23	203	36	7	0	4	13	15	54	8	3	.209/.275/.313
2017	TEX	MLB	24	440	75	15	2	6	22	44	109	29	8	.269/.347/.367
2018	TEX	MLB	25	393	52	14	1	2	22	43	83	20	4	.216/.310/.281
2019	TEX	MLB	26	457	61	17	2	8	36	47	104	24	7	.239/.324/.354

Breakout: 11% Improve: 60% Collapse: 11% Attrition: 17% MLB: 95%
Comparables: Marvin Benard, Willy Taveras, Carlos Gomez

The Rangers began 2018 with DeShields as their everyday leadoff man and center fielder, which made it a really bad time for him to break his hamate. His bat never looked right after that, so hopefully a full offseason will make a difference for the second-generation big leaguer. On the upside, his oft-maligned defense took major strides early in the season, though it did regress a bit as the dog days dragged on. Between the hamate, a concussion and the rise of Joey Gallo: Center Fielder, Jon Daniels declined to commit to DeShields as the Rangers' starter this season, instead saying he would have an opportunity to compete for a starting job. Now the question is whether he'll be competing for center field, left field or another team altogether.

YEAR	TEAM	LVL	AGE	PA	DRC+	VORP	BABIP	BRR	FRAA	WARP
2016	ROU	AAA	23	249	110	15.5	.349	2.4	CF(42): -5.7, LF(7): -1.9	0.1
2016	TEX	MLB	23	203	64	-0.9	.272	2.0	CF(33): 1.1, LF(26): -1.4	-0.1
2017	TEX	MLB	24	440	86	14.1	.358	7.6	LF(60): 4.3, CF(51): -0.5	1.7
2018	TEX	MLB	25	393	73	1.1	.280	3.4	CF(102): 10.3	1.5
2019	TEX	MLB	26	457	81	12.0	.293	2.5	CF 0	1.0

Delino DeShields, continued

Batted Ball Distribution

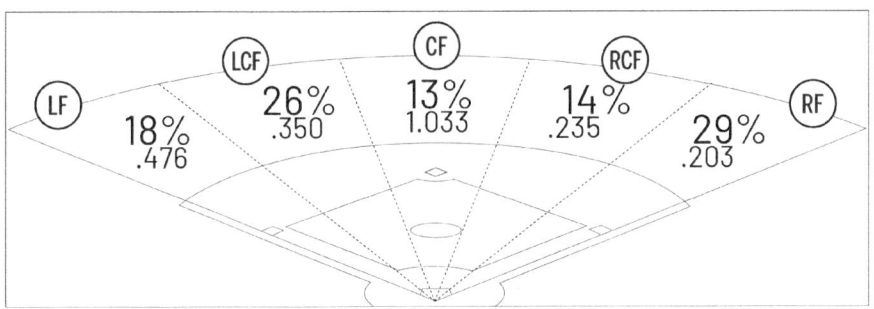

Strike Zone vs LHP   **Strike Zone vs RHP**

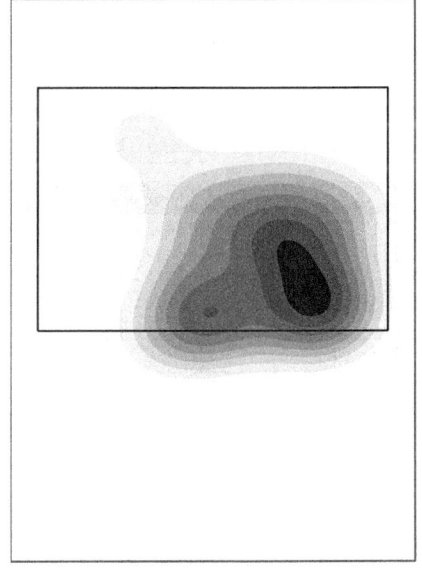
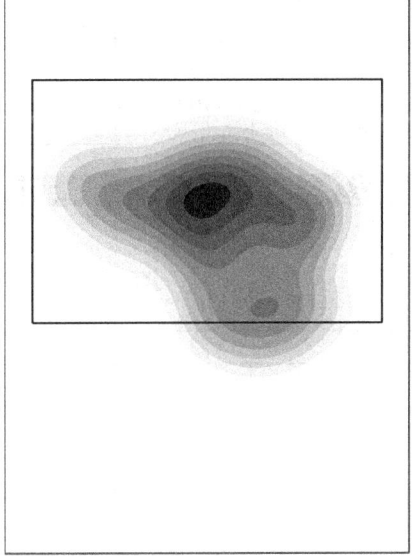

Logan Forsythe 2B

Born: 01/14/87   Age: 32   Bats: R   Throws: R
Height: 6'1"   Weight: 205   Origin: Round 1, 2008 Draft (#46 overall)

YEAR	TEAM	LVL	AGE	PA	R	2B	3B	HR	RBI	BB	K	SB	CS	AVG/OBP/SLG
2016	TBA	MLB	29	567	76	24	4	20	52	46	127	6	6	.264/.333/.444
2017	LAN	MLB	30	439	56	19	0	6	36	69	109	3	2	.224/.351/.327
2018	LAN	MLB	31	211	18	10	0	2	13	17	43	2	0	.207/.270/.290
2018	MIN	MLB	31	205	19	6	0	0	14	24	40	1	0	.258/.356/.292
2019	TEX	MLB	32	162	18	8	1	3	16	18	36	1	1	.248/.340/.383

Breakout: 1%   Improve: 34%   Collapse: 13%   Attrition: 6%   MLB: 93%
Comparables: Orlando Hudson, Mark Ellis, Mike Sharperson

Forsythe saw 1,700 pitches in 2018, and 53.2 percent of them were in the strike zone. No batter who saw even 1,000 pitches had as many of them pass through the zone. That's who Forsythe is right now: the least-feared hitter in baseball. He's well past the line between patient and passive, and since he's managed just 45 extra-base hits over the last two seasons, that's probably the right strategy. Forsythe's best chance at retaining utility is to keep battling his way to the occasional walk. At this stage of his career, even that won't punch his ticket to Lineupville very often. He's not a good enough defender to make that profile work, especially if pitchers keep seeing a gigantic cartoon steak when they look in at him in the box.

YEAR	TEAM	LVL	AGE	PA	DRC+	VORP	BABIP	BRR	FRAA	WARP
2016	TBA	MLB	29	567	113	24.9	.314	0.6	2B(118): -7.9	1.8
2017	LAN	MLB	30	439	93	14.1	.299	0.5	2B(80): 4.8, 3B(42): -0.1	1.5
2018	LAN	MLB	31	211	78	-6.3	.255	0.0	2B(51): 5.7, 3B(12): 1.3	0.8
2018	MIN	MLB	31	205	80	3.6	.333	1.5	2B(48): -5.5	-0.3
2019	TEX	MLB	32	162	99	5.4	.309	-0.2	3B 0, 2B 0	0.5

Logan Forsythe, continued

Batted Ball Distribution

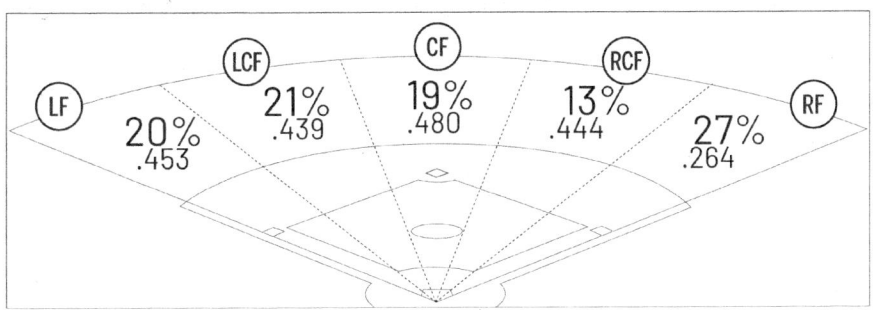

Strike Zone vs LHP

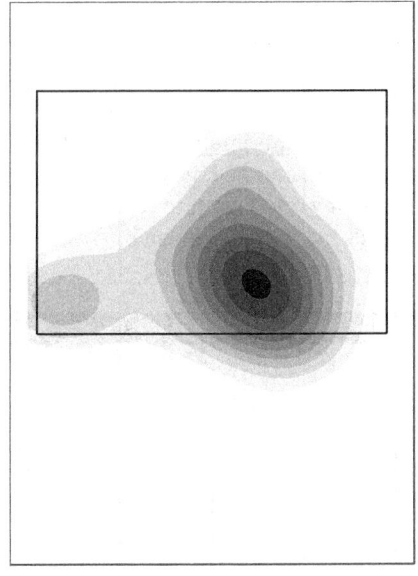

Strike Zone vs RHP

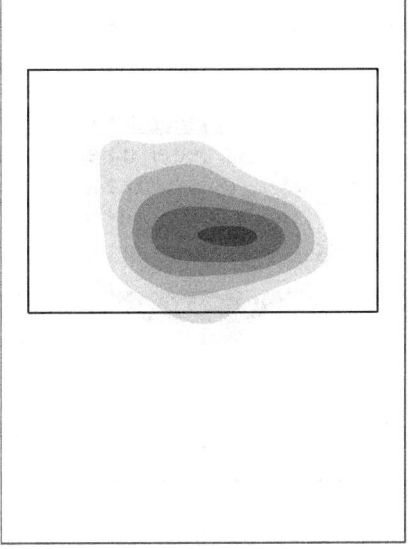

Texas Rangers 2019

Joey Gallo LF

Born: 11/19/93   Age: 25   Bats: L   Throws: R
Height: 6'5"   Weight: 235   Origin: Round 1, 2012 Draft (#39 overall)

YEAR	TEAM	LVL	AGE	PA	R	2B	3B	HR	RBI	BB	K	SB	CS	AVG/OBP/SLG
2016	ROU	AAA	22	433	71	17	6	25	66	68	150	2	0	.240/.367/.529
2016	TEX	MLB	22	30	2	0	0	1	1	5	19	1	0	.040/.200/.160
2017	TEX	MLB	23	532	85	18	3	41	80	75	196	7	2	.209/.333/.537
2018	TEX	MLB	24	577	82	24	1	40	92	74	207	3	4	.206/.312/.498
2019	TEX	MLB	25	577	82	23	3	35	92	72	196	5	2	.222/.326/.492

Breakout: 8%   Improve: 52%   Collapse: 13%   Attrition: 11%   MLB: 95%
Comparables: Miguel Sano, Kyle Schwarber, Kris Bryant

Gallo is the baseball equivalent of an angry monster truck that tops out at 100 mph and runs on gold-infused thrice-refined jet fuel harvested from only the southernmost tip of the Cape of Good Hope by unionized leprechauns. Sure, it's a tremendously entertaining time watching the Michael Bay-directed mayhem and destruction he wreaks upon baseballs, but how long is the team going to be able to afford the strikeouts? Gallo is never going to be a Tesla or a Prius (and the Rangers shouldn't want him to be), but as he matures, perhaps he can transition to a more reasonable number of strikeouts, like 150-160. Of course, that's the easy thing to point out about Gallo. The more fascinating issue to watch in 2019 is whether the Rangers continue the experiment of playing him in center field. He's a better athlete than many realize, and he has the tools to succeed, but it's possible the team will decide they don't want to risk the additional wear and tear on the monster truck's body (and offensive production).

YEAR	TEAM	LVL	AGE	PA	DRC+	VORP	BABIP	BRR	FRAA	WARP
2016	ROU	AAA	22	433	141	40.0	.330	2.1	3B(44): 4.5, 1B(32): 1.4	2.9
2016	TEX	MLB	22	30	44	-2.8	.000	-0.1	3B(5): 0.2, 1B(1): 0.1	-0.1
2017	TEX	MLB	23	532	123	27.6	.250	0.5	3B(72): -1.8, 1B(59): 0.5	3.1
2018	TEX	MLB	24	577	116	20.7	.249	1.9	LF(85): -6.3, 1B(35): 3.1	2.7
2019	TEX	MLB	25	577	111	25.9	.278	-0.4	LF -4, CF 0	2.1

Joey Gallo, continued

Batted Ball Distribution

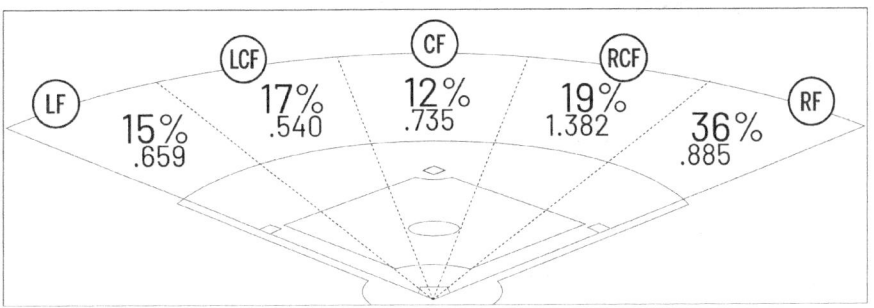

LF	LCF	CF	RCF	RF
15% .659	17% .540	12% .735	19% 1.382	36% .885

Strike Zone vs LHP

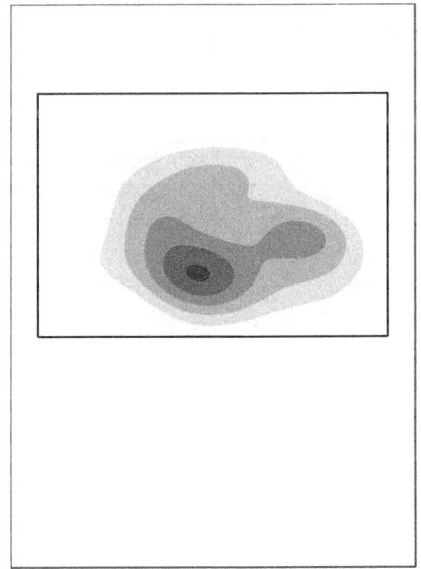

Strike Zone vs RHP

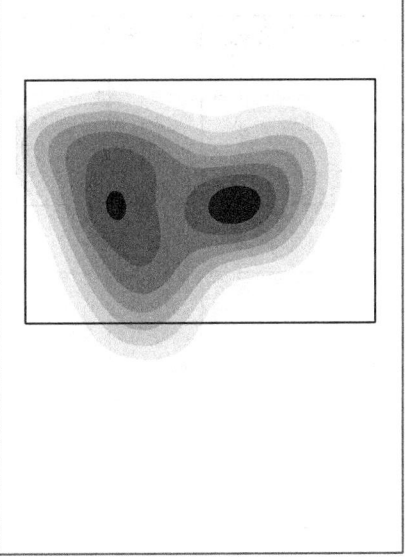

Ronald Guzman 1B

Born: 10/20/94 Age: 24 Bats: L Throws: L
Height: 6'5" Weight: 225 Origin: International Free Agent, 2011

YEAR	TEAM	LVL	AGE	PA	R	2B	3B	HR	RBI	BB	K	SB	CS	AVG/OBP/SLG
2016	FRI	AA	21	416	51	16	5	15	56	33	82	2	1	.288/.348/.477
2016	ROU	AAA	21	95	9	5	1	1	11	6	23	0	1	.216/.266/.330
2017	ROU	AAA	22	527	78	22	3	12	62	47	85	4	1	.298/.372/.434
2018	TEX	MLB	23	428	46	18	2	16	58	33	121	1	0	.235/.306/.416
2019	TEX	MLB	24	474	52	19	3	15	54	34	108	1	0	.242/.307/.405

Breakout: 7% Improve: 48% Collapse: 3% Attrition: 22% MLB: 68%
Comparables: Kendrys Morales, James Loney, Joey Votto

He's super bendy, can do the splits, out-danced Astros mascot Orbit and hit a career-high (at any level) in home runs in 2018. There was some concern that he would not muster enough power and pull-side hard contact to stick at first base, but Guzman acquitted himself well in his rookie campaign, allowing the Rangers to tinker with putting Joey Gallo all over the outfield.

YEAR	TEAM	LVL	AGE	PA	DRC+	VORP	BABIP	BRR	FRAA	WARP
2016	FRI	AA	21	416	128	16.6	.331	-2.5	1B(95): 4.0	1.0
2016	ROU	AAA	21	95	67	-5.4	.281	-1.6	1B(20): -1.6	-0.7
2017	ROU	AAA	22	527	117	20.4	.342	-0.3	1B(118): -1.6	0.9
2018	TEX	MLB	23	428	92	3.0	.299	1.9	1B(117): 1.9	0.6
2019	TEX	MLB	24	474	87	3.2	.288	-0.5	1B 0	0.1

Ronald Guzman, continued

Batted Ball Distribution

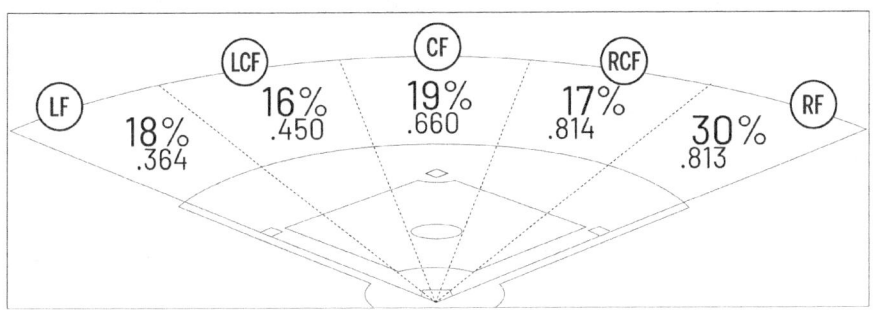

Strike Zone vs LHP

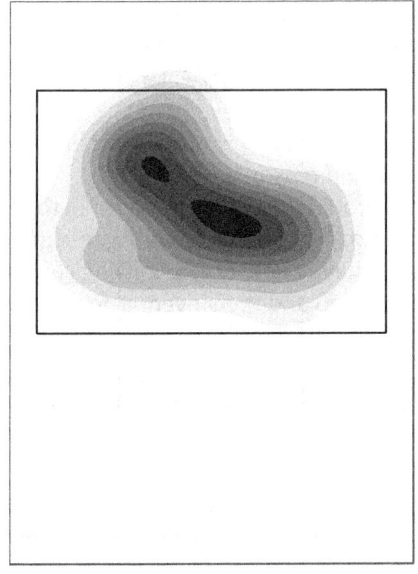

Strike Zone vs RHP

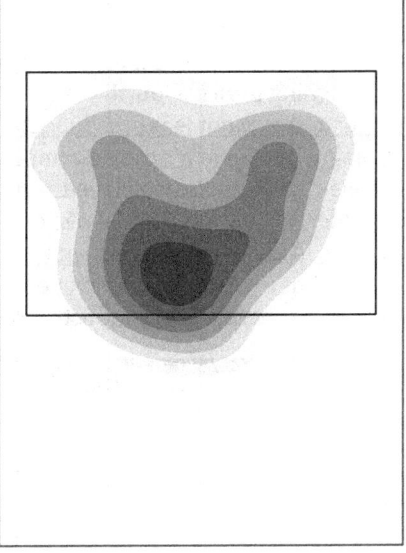

Isiah Kiner-Falefa 3B/C

Born: 03/23/95 Age: 24 Bats: R Throws: R
Height: 5'10" Weight: 176 Origin: Round 4, 2013 Draft (#130 overall)

YEAR	TEAM	LVL	AGE	PA	R	2B	3B	HR	RBI	BB	K	SB	CS	AVG/OBP/SLG
2016	FRI	AA	21	457	55	8	2	0	27	41	51	6	6	.256/.341/.286
2017	FRI	AA	22	570	58	31	3	5	48	41	72	17	6	.288/.350/.390
2018	TEX	MLB	23	396	43	18	2	4	34	28	62	7	5	.261/.325/.357
2019	TEX	MLB	24	363	38	15	2	7	36	30	57	6	3	.254/.325/.378

Breakout: 13% Improve: 49% Collapse: 2% Attrition: 15% MLB: 67%
Comparables: Willy Aybar, Blake DeWitt, Ronald Torreyes

Do you remember the '90s TV show *The Pretender*? It was about a guy named Jarod (pronounced like "Jared"), who was a savant and could quickly master the terminology and skills needed to blend in at any job as

YEAR	TEAM	P. COUNT	FRM RUNS	BLK RUNS	THRW RUNS	TOT RUNS
2017	FRI	4556	-1.1	-0.8	0.0	-1.7
2018	TEX	4896	-9.9	-1.0	0.0	-10.9
2019	TEX	9669	-15.9	-1.8	0.1	-17.6

he evaded capture by a mysterious organization called "The Centre." One week, he would be a doctor, scanning through a book and then performing a complex surgery, and then the next week, he was a rodeo clown. Kiner-Falefa did not start catching until his fourth year as a professional and played just 69 games at catcher in the minor leagues, but donned the tools of ignorance in 35 of his 111 big-league games in his rookie campaign, and did reasonably well. The Hawaiian Army Knife also played second base, shortstop and third base in the bigs (after playing all of the above plus left field, center field and one game at first base in the minor leagues). If the Rangers have another cow-milking contest in 2019, Kiner-Falefa will watch one YouTube video and then invent a new method that becomes the industry standard.

YEAR	TEAM	LVL	AGE	PA	DRC+	VORP	BABIP	BRR	FRAA	WARP
2016	FRI	AA	21	457	97	9.0	.293	-1.0	3B(44): 10.2, C(31): -6.2	1.0
2017	FRI	AA	22	570	120	35.4	.325	0.2	3B(50): 6.4, 2B(37): 4.2	3.1
2018	TEX	MLB	23	396	86	4.0	.306	-0.6	3B(46): 3.4, C(35): -10.1	0.1
2019	TEX	MLB	24	363	88	9.9	.286	-0.2	C -18, 3B 2	-0.7

Isiah Kiner-Falefa, continued

Batted Ball Distribution

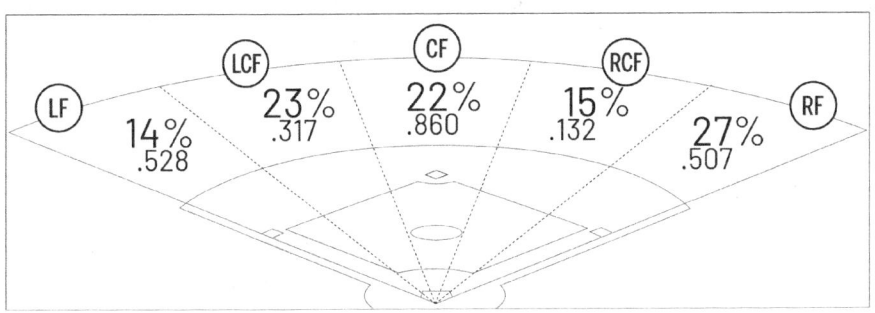

Strike Zone vs LHP

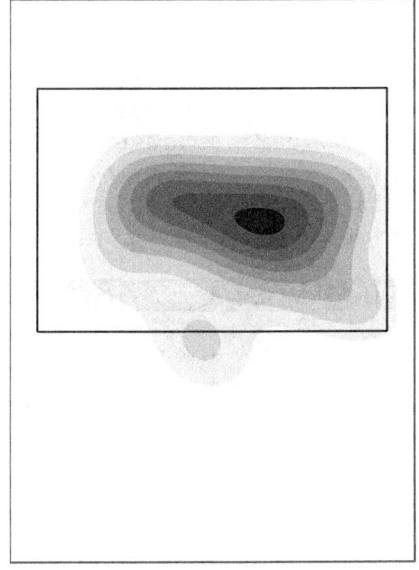

Strike Zone vs RHP

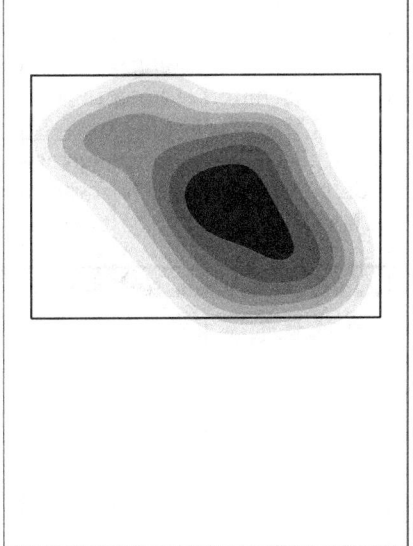

Jeff Mathis C

Born: 03/31/83   Age: 36   Bats: R   Throws: R
Height: 6'0"   Weight: 205   Origin: Round 1, 2001 Draft (#33 overall)

YEAR	TEAM	LVL	AGE	PA	R	2B	3B	HR	RBI	BB	K	SB	CS	AVG/OBP/SLG
2016	MIA	MLB	33	132	12	4	1	2	15	4	36	0	0	.238/.267/.333
2017	ARI	MLB	34	203	13	10	2	2	11	14	61	1	0	.215/.277/.323
2018	ARI	MLB	35	218	15	9	1	1	20	20	66	0	0	.200/.272/.272
2019	TEX	MLB	36	315	29	14	2	5	29	23	85	1	0	.228/.291/.344

Breakout: 1%   Improve: 32%   Collapse: 10%   Attrition: 37%   MLB: 80%
Comparables: Paul Bako, Jose Molina, Mike Matheny

YEAR	TEAM	P. COUNT	FRM RUNS	BLK RUNS	THRW RUNS	TOT RUNS
2016	MIA	5038	7.9	0.8	-0.1	8.9
2017	ARI	7723	8.9	-0.7	1.1	8.9
2018	ARI	8583	11.8	2.3	0.0	14.1
2019	TEX	12261	14.3	1.2	0.4	15.9

In recent years, advanced defensive metrics have confirmed what the eye test and Mike Scioscia's love always said about Mathis, who's tallied +97 Fielding Runs Above Average for his career despite starting fewer than 80 games in 13 of his 14 seasons. An elite pitch framer and blocker with a decent arm, Mathis has also earned rave reviews for handling every pitching staff he's ever worked with. He was among the majors' worst hitters last season, which has been the case for nearly his entire career, yet Mathis snagged a two-year, $6.25 million deal to serve as the Rangers' backup catcher through age 36. He'll retire with zero Gold Glove awards, because those go to starters rather than backups, but on a per-game basis Mathis is one of the best defensive catchers of the past two decades.

YEAR	TEAM	LVL	AGE	PA	DRC+	VORP	BABIP	BRR	FRAA	WARP
2016	MIA	MLB	33	132	72	1.9	.318	0.0	C(38): 9.1	1.1
2017	ARI	MLB	34	203	59	-1.5	.309	0.4	C(58): 10.2	1.0
2018	ARI	MLB	35	218	63	-3.4	.292	-0.4	C(63): 18.5, P(1): 0.0	2.0
2019	TEX	MLB	36	315	71	3.8	.304	-0.4	C 18	2.0

Jeff Mathis, continued

Batted Ball Distribution

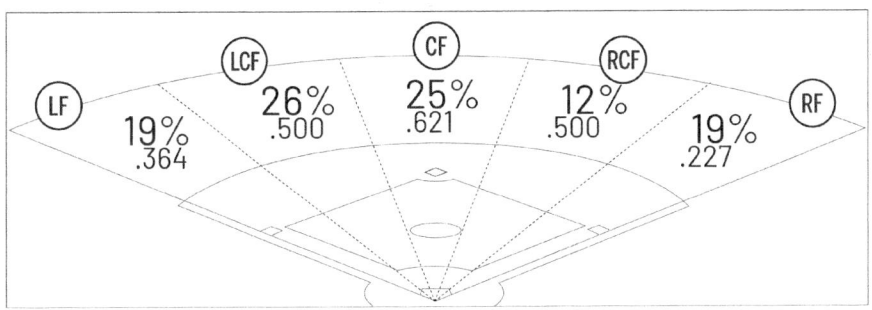

Strike Zone vs LHP

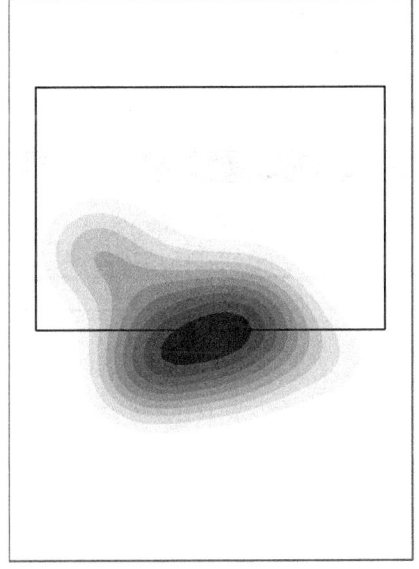

Strike Zone vs RHP

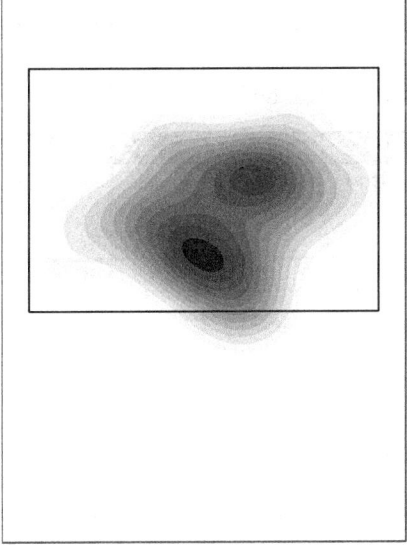

Nomar Mazara RF

Born: 04/26/95   Age: 24   Bats: L   Throws: L
Height: 6'4"   Weight: 215   Origin: International Free Agent, 2011

YEAR	TEAM	LVL	AGE	PA	R	2B	3B	HR	RBI	BB	K	SB	CS	AVG/OBP/SLG
2016	TEX	MLB	21	568	59	13	3	20	64	39	112	0	2	.266/.320/.419
2017	TEX	MLB	22	616	64	30	2	20	101	55	127	2	2	.253/.323/.422
2018	TEX	MLB	23	536	61	25	1	20	77	40	116	1	0	.258/.317/.436
2019	TEX	MLB	24	563	64	25	3	19	71	46	111	2	1	.261/.327/.434

Breakout: 5%   Improve: 55%   Collapse: 15%   Attrition: 7%   MLB: 98%
Comparables: Tony Tarasco, Bob Elliott, Nick Markakis

Here is a set of statistics: 1. Mazara has a 20 percent homer-per-fly ball rate. That's the 21st-best in baseball among qualifiers. 2. Mazara has a 27 percent fly-ball rate. That's 12th-lowest in baseball. One of the problems was that Mazara swung at too many pitches outside the strike zone (34 percent). Sure, he made contact with a reasonable percentage of those (64), but it wasn't the good kind of contact. In his defense, he injured his thumb just before the All-Star break, and his second-half numbers suffered greatly, almost certainly as a result. Additionally, he's just now on the verge of being 24 years old. There's still time to correct the issue, and Mazara's a whip-smart baseball player, playing for a big-league organization, with an analytics department and everything.

YEAR	TEAM	LVL	AGE	PA	DRC+	VORP	BABIP	BRR	FRAA	WARP
2016	TEX	MLB	21	568	100	4.6	.299	-4.1	RF(112): 11.2, LF(38): -1.3	1.8
2017	TEX	MLB	22	616	91	0.8	.293	-2.4	RF(92): -6.2, LF(47): 0.8	-0.1
2018	TEX	MLB	23	536	98	5.6	.298	-1.2	RF(113): -10.2, LF(2): -0.2	-0.2
2019	TEX	MLB	24	563	98	12.9	.297	-0.9	RF -7	0.6

Nomar Mazara, continued

Batted Ball Distribution

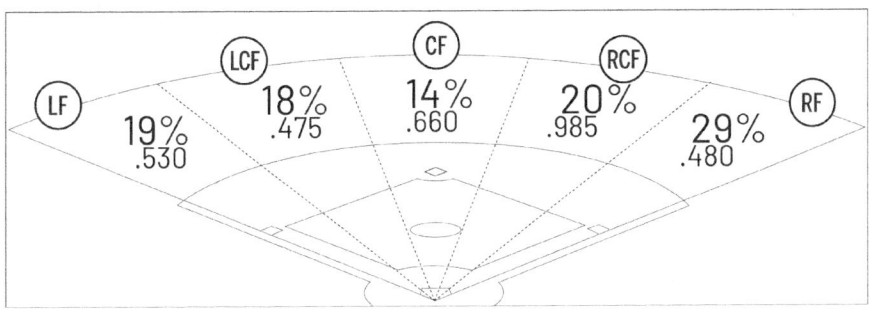

Strike Zone vs LHP

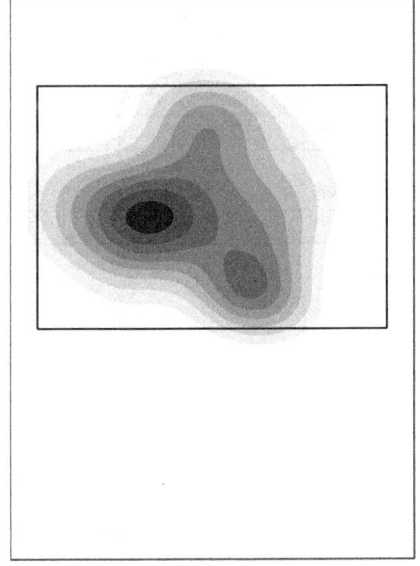

Strike Zone vs RHP

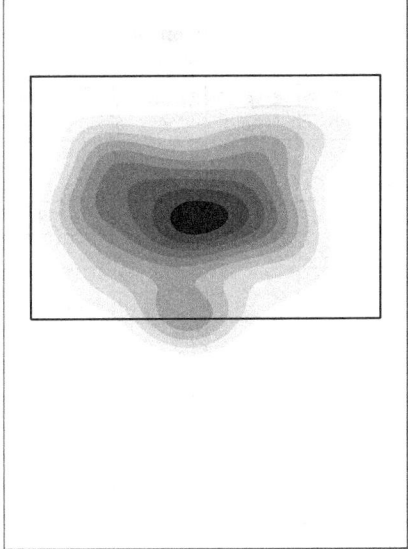

Rougned Odor 2B

Born: 02/03/94   Age: 25   Bats: L   Throws: R
Height: 5'11"   Weight: 195   Origin: International Free Agent, 2011

YEAR	TEAM	LVL	AGE	PA	R	2B	3B	HR	RBI	BB	K	SB	CS	AVG/OBP/SLG
2016	TEX	MLB	22	632	89	33	4	33	88	19	135	14	7	.271/.296/.502
2017	TEX	MLB	23	651	79	21	3	30	75	32	162	15	6	.204/.252/.397
2018	TEX	MLB	24	535	76	23	2	18	63	43	127	12	12	.253/.326/.424
2019	*TEX*	*MLB*	*25*	*594*	*83*	*28*	*3*	*23*	*68*	*38*	*132*	*13*	*9*	*.249/.306/.439*

Breakout: 6%   Improve: 59%   Collapse: 5%   Attrition: 8%   MLB: 98%
Comparables: Gordon Beckham, Robinson Cano, Jonathan Schoop

Odor runs like a burlap sack full of furious badgers. Last year, the first few paragraphs of the Rangers team essay waxed philosophical about patience and vision as they pertained to Odor. There's an irony, then, in noting that the Rangers' patience with the second baseman paid off for an extended stretch in 2018. Yes, his home run numbers dipped, but they did so while he increased his slugging percentage. There's a tired joke to be made here about Odor's 2017 being *flat*, and 2018 being more *well-rounded*, because he *drove* the ball more, but we'll let you put that one together. (Tire. It's a tire pun. A tired pun.)

YEAR	TEAM	LVL	AGE	PA	DRC+	VORP	BABIP	BRR	FRAA	WARP
2016	TEX	MLB	22	632	111	22.5	.297	-0.2	2B(146): 5.7	3.3
2017	TEX	MLB	23	651	75	-9.5	.224	1.3	2B(158): 6.2	0.7
2018	TEX	MLB	24	535	97	14.8	.305	1.0	2B(127): 7.5	2.4
2019	*TEX*	*MLB*	*25*	*594*	*94*	*16.3*	*.284*	*-0.5*	*2B 4*	*1.9*

Rougned Odor, continued

Batted Ball Distribution

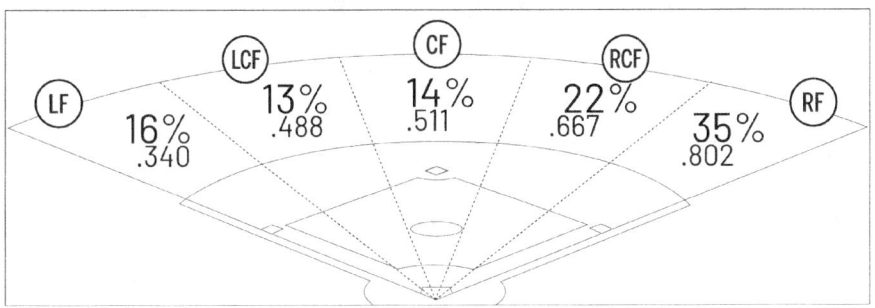

Strike Zone vs LHP   Strike Zone vs RHP

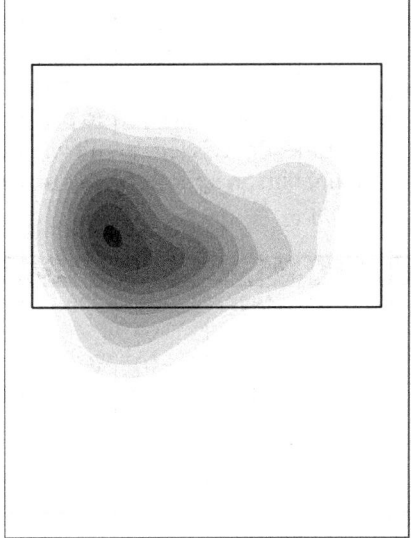

Hunter Pence RF

Born: 04/13/83 Age: 36 Bats: R Throws: R
Height: 6'4" Weight: 230 Origin: Round 2, 2004 Draft (#64 overall)

YEAR	TEAM	LVL	AGE	PA	R	2B	3B	HR	RBI	BB	K	SB	CS	AVG/OBP/SLG
2016	SFN	MLB	33	442	58	23	1	13	57	43	95	1	1	.289/.357/.451
2017	SFN	MLB	34	539	55	13	5	13	67	40	102	2	3	.260/.315/.385
2018	SAC	AAA	35	111	11	4	0	1	13	6	24	0	0	.301/.342/.369
2018	SFN	MLB	35	248	19	11	1	4	24	11	59	5	1	.226/.258/.332
2019	TEX	MLB	36	167	17	7	1	4	18	13	36	1	1	.257/.317/.395

Breakout: 0% Improve: 22% Collapse: 19% Attrition: 13% MLB: 76%
Comparables: Johnny Dickshot, Jose Cruz, Brian Jordan

Desperate times call for desperate measures, so when a slumping Pence found himself rehabbing a thumb injury with Triple-A Sacramento in May, he seized the opportunity to alter his distinctive swing. The long-time fan favorite for lumbering movements and wacky faces that belied outstanding athleticism and dynamic tools, Pence stood more upright in the box, lowered his hands and used a more deliberate knee-lift stride reminiscent of Justin Turner's. Although the change didn't manifest in an offensive revival, Pence led the Giants with five batted balls over 110 mph, showing there's plenty of thunder left in his stick. He went all-in on the Turnerization in the offseason, visiting with Turner's coach Doug Latta, a last-ditch effort to prolong his career as he tests free agency for the first time. Pence's legs aren't what they once were, but his intangibles should net him an opportunity as an extra outfielder if he rediscovers some of his old pop.

YEAR	TEAM	LVL	AGE	PA	DRC+	VORP	BABIP	BRR	FRAA	WARP
2016	SFN	MLB	33	442	107	25.8	.348	-1.8	RF(102): -1.2	1.0
2017	SFN	MLB	34	539	89	17.3	.301	4.4	RF(125): 2.0	1.1
2018	SAC	AAA	35	111	95	1.9	.380	-0.1	RF(12): 0.1, LF(11): 0.2	0.1
2018	SFN	MLB	35	248	66	-2.7	.282	0.4	LF(44): -3.1, RF(12): -1.2	-0.8
2019	TEX	MLB	36	167	85	1.6	.303	-0.1	LF 1	0.2

Hunter Pence, continued

Batted Ball Distribution

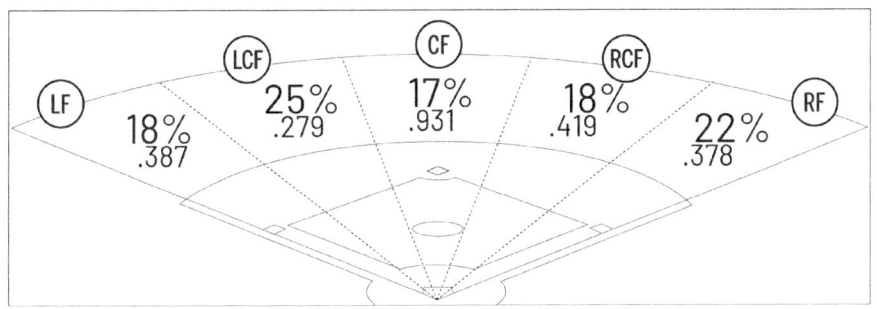

Strike Zone vs LHP

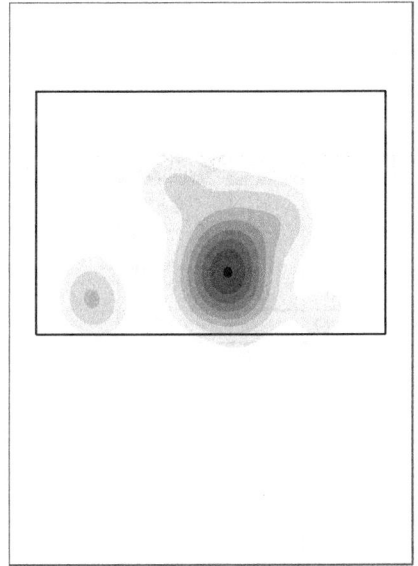

Strike Zone vs RHP

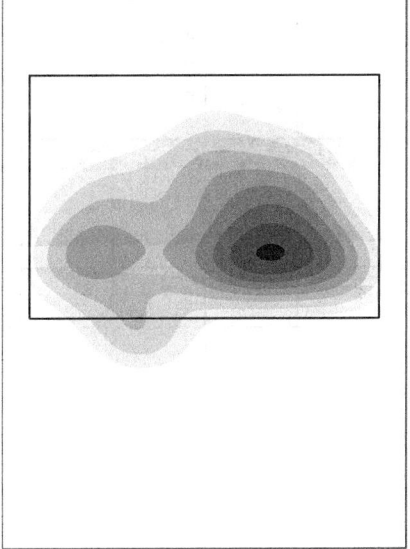

Carlos Tocci CF

Born: 08/23/95   Age: 23   Bats: R   Throws: R
Height: 6'2"   Weight: 160   Origin: International Free Agent, 2011

YEAR	TEAM	LVL	AGE	PA	R	2B	3B	HR	RBI	BB	K	SB	CS	AVG/OBP/SLG
2016	CLR	A+	20	556	66	26	2	3	50	34	76	13	6	.284/.331/.362
2017	REA	AA	21	474	59	19	7	2	48	29	66	4	5	.307/.362/.398
2017	LEH	AAA	21	54	2	0	0	1	4	1	11	0	0	.189/.204/.245
2018	TEX	MLB	22	135	11	3	2	0	5	7	39	0	3	.225/.271/.283
2019	TEX	MLB	23	58	6	2	0	1	5	4	14	0	0	.208/.276/.302

Breakout: 10%   Improve: 18%   Collapse: 0%   Attrition: 7%   MLB: 18%
Comparables: Andrew Stevenson, Rosell Herrera, Ender Inciarte

For the first half of 2018, all anyone could say about Tocci was "why is this guy on the roster?" And the only answer was "because he's a Rule 5 pick." To which Person A (usually on Twitter) would say, "Yah. I know." Kind of rude, but they had a point: Tocci was hitting .086 at the All-Star break. But after that point, the defense-first center fielder hit .282 in his last 94 plate appearances. That doesn't mean he's going to be the Rangers' starting center fielder in 2019—he can now be sent to the minor leagues after having spent a full season on the big-league roster, and he did slug just .365 over those last 38 games—but it does help to justify having kept the now-23-year-old on the roster all season.

YEAR	TEAM	LVL	AGE	PA	DRC+	VORP	BABIP	BRR	FRAA	WARP
2016	CLR	A+	20	556	113	20.6	.324	1.7	CF(122): -0.6, RF(4): -0.2	1.4
2017	REA	AA	21	474	112	23.8	.356	1.5	CF(94): -5.2, RF(14): 3.3	1.1
2017	LEH	AAA	21	54	30	-5.0	.220	0.0	CF(11): 3.5, LF(3): -0.3	0.0
2018	TEX	MLB	22	135	60	-5.1	.329	-0.1	CF(47): -0.7, RF(10): -0.6	-0.3
2019	TEX	MLB	23	58	60	-0.9	.271	-0.1	CF 0, RF 0	-0.1

Carlos Tocci, continued

Batted Ball Distribution

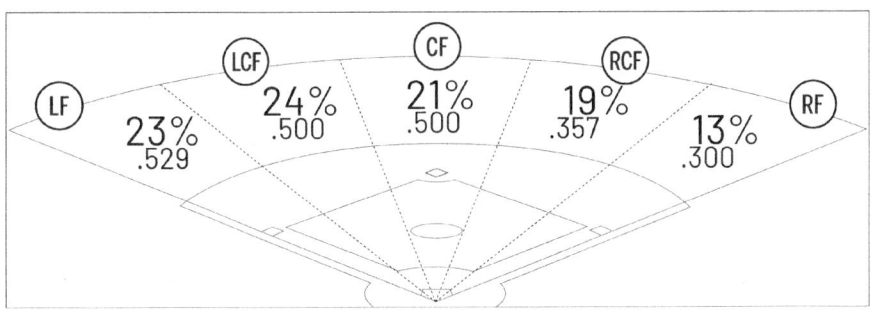

Strike Zone vs LHP

Strike Zone vs RHP

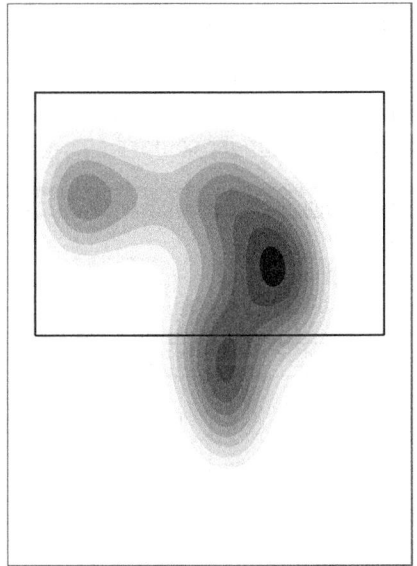
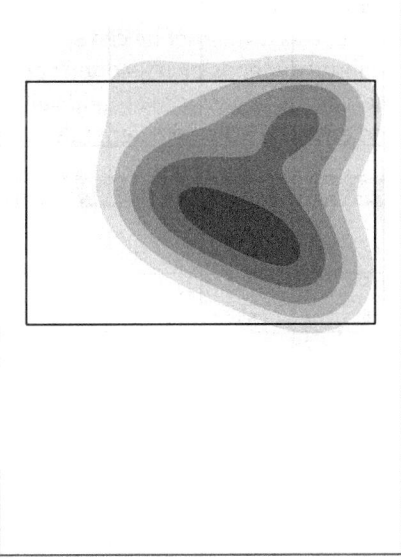

Texas Rangers 2019

Patrick Wisdom 3B
Born: 08/27/91   Age: 27   Bats: R   Throws: R
Height: 6'2"   Weight: 220   Origin: Round 1, 2012 Draft (#52 overall)

YEAR	TEAM	LVL	AGE	PA	R	2B	3B	HR	RBI	BB	K	SB	CS	AVG/OBP/SLG
2016	MEM	AAA	24	295	29	20	1	5	30	26	73	5	1	.233/.303/.374
2017	MEM	AAA	25	506	68	25	1	31	89	38	149	2	2	.243/.310/.507
2018	MEM	AAA	26	421	65	24	1	15	61	43	112	11	2	.288/.363/.480
2018	SLN	MLB	26	58	11	1	0	4	10	6	19	2	1	.260/.362/.520
2019	TEX	MLB	27	150	18	7	1	6	19	10	45	2	1	.219/.280/.416

Breakout: 2%   Improve: 23%   Collapse: 7%   Attrition: 18%   MLB: 37%
Comparables: David Freese, Patrick Kivlehan, Mike Olt

Just a fortnight shy of his 27th birthday, Wisdom finally punched his ticket to the majors. Before that, he punched many, many bus and meal tickets across the country, racking up over 1,200 plate appearances in Triple-A Memphis alone. He also punched out many, many times, and he continued to do so once he reached The Show. Wisdom has good power, but whether it's enough depends on how often he can make contact. He's made gradual improvements in plate discipline, but whether he can sustain those against big leaguers with any regularity depends on how often can make contact. He's a serviceable third baseman, but doesn't really add value with the glove, so even whether he's good enough in the field depends on how often he can make contact.

YEAR	TEAM	LVL	AGE	PA	DRC+	VORP	BABIP	BRR	FRAA	WARP
2016	MEM	AAA	24	295	80	4.3	.298	-2.6	3B(65): 5.6, 1B(4): 0.0	0.1
2017	MEM	AAA	25	506	104	32.0	.286	1.5	3B(113): 0.1, 1B(8): 0.5	1.6
2018	MEM	AAA	26	421	122	37.5	.371	4.9	3B(93): -5.2, 1B(7): 0.5	1.9
2018	SLN	MLB	26	58	83	5.3	.333	0.0	3B(13): -0.4, 1B(4): -0.4	0.0
2019	TEX	MLB	27	150	84	0.6	.283	0.0	3B -1, 1B 0	0.0

Patrick Wisdom, continued

Batted Ball Distribution

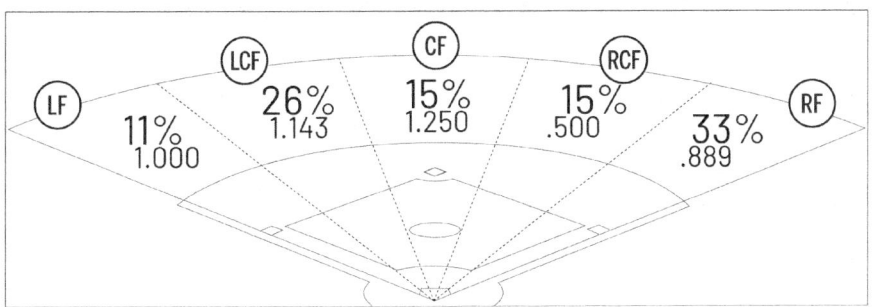

Strike Zone vs LHP

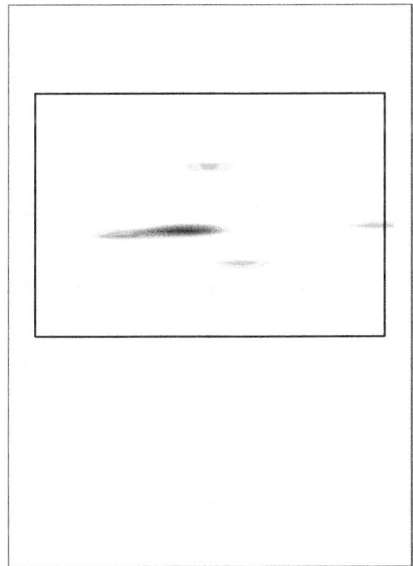

Strike Zone vs RHP

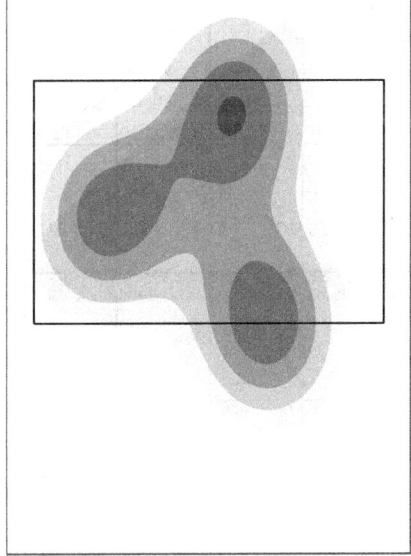

Texas Rangers 2019

Matt Bush RHP
Born: 02/08/86   Age: 33   Bats: R   Throws: R
Height: 5'9"   Weight: 180   Origin: Round 1, 2004 Draft (#1 overall)

YEAR	TEAM	LVL	AGE	W	L	SV	G	GS	IP	H	HR	BB/9	K/9	K	GB%	BABIP
2016	FRI	AA	30	0	2	5	12	0	17	9	2	2.1	9.5	18	42%	.184
2016	TEX	MLB	30	7	2	1	58	0	61²	44	4	2.0	8.9	61	45%	.245
2017	TEX	MLB	31	3	4	10	57	0	52¹	57	7	3.3	10.0	58	39%	.329
2018	ROU	AAA	32	1	1	0	8	0	9	9	0	4.0	14.0	14	55%	.409
2018	TEX	MLB	32	0	0	0	21	0	23	23	3	5.5	7.4	19	48%	.286
2019	TEX	MLB	33	2	1	2	32	0	34¹	33	4	3.9	8.4	32	44%	.293

Breakout: 23%   Improve: 40%   Collapse: 28%   Attrition: 13%   MLB: 86%
Comparables: Kevin Jepsen, Craig Stammen, Jason Frasor

Bush's 2018 season was like one of those days you forget your coffee, so you have to make an extra stop on the way to work, but because the new coffee is in a cheap disposable cup with a lid that cost the corporation half a cent, the whole thing buckles and spills on your pants as you're getting out of the car. Then you're in the bathroom trying to wash out the stain at the sink and someone walks in on you, which startles you, causing you to bump your head on the hand dryer. You're woozy now, and you stumble on the wet floor, but at the last second you reach out and grab the sink for support, which causes you to injure your UCL badly enough to require surgery, which will cost you the first half of the 2019 season. And it's then and only then that you get to your desk and see the note: Your contract is not being renewed, and you're unemployed. At least it's not Tommy John surgery?

YEAR	TEAM	LVL	AGE	WHIP	ERA	DRA	WARP	MPH	FB%	WHF	CSP
2016	FRI	AA	30	0.76	2.65	2.70	0.4				
2016	TEX	MLB	30	0.94	2.48	3.35	1.1	99.7	68.1	14.4	51.2
2017	TEX	MLB	31	1.45	3.78	5.53	-0.2	99.2	68.9	13.3	51
2018	ROU	AAA	32	1.44	2.00	2.26	0.3				
2018	TEX	MLB	32	1.61	4.70	6.72	-0.5	98.1	63.4	10.1	48.7
2019	TEX	MLB	33	1.38	4.55	4.50	0.2	98.0	66.5	12.7	49.5

Matt Bush, continued

Pitch Shape vs LHH

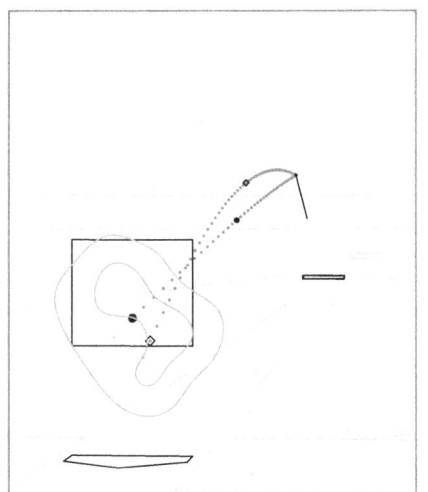

Pitch Shape vs RHH

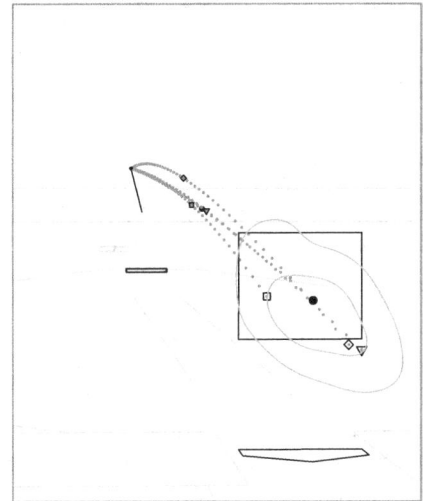

Type	Frequency	Velocity	H Movement	V Movement
● Fastball	54.7%	96.8 [114]	-3.1 [116]	-9.9 [118]
☐ Sinker	8.7%	96.5 [120]	-10.6 [117]	-12.7 [125]
+ Cutter				
▲ Changeup	0.2%	84.2 [95]	-15.2 [79]	-29.2 [95]
× Splitter				
▽ Slider	13.3%	92.4 [135]	4.3 [98]	-21.9 [133]
◇ Curveball	23.1%	80.6 [108]	10.2 [110]	-46.1 [104]
⊕ Slow Curveball				
✳ Knuckleball				
▼ Screwball				

Jesse Chavez   RHP

Born: 08/21/83   Age: 35   Bats: R   Throws: R
Height: 6'2"   Weight: 175   Origin: Round 42, 2002 Draft (#1252 overall)

YEAR	TEAM	LVL	AGE	W	L	SV	G	GS	IP	H	HR	BB/9	K/9	K	GB%	BABIP
2016	TOR	MLB	32	1	2	0	39	0	41^1	43	9	2.2	9.1	42	46%	.309
2016	LAN	MLB	32	1	0	0	23	0	25^2	28	3	2.8	7.4	21	39%	.325
2017	ANA	MLB	33	7	11	0	38	21	138	148	28	2.9	7.8	119	42%	.306
2018	TEX	MLB	34	3	1	1	30	0	56^1	58	10	1.9	8.0	50	45%	.296
2018	CHN	MLB	34	2	1	4	32	0	39	26	3	1.2	9.7	42	43%	.247
2019	TEX	MLB	35	3	3	0	59	0	62	61	9	3.0	8.7	61	43%	.297

Breakout: 17%   Improve: 38%   Collapse: 18%   Attrition: 7%   MLB: 80%
Comparables: Jim Bunning, Larry French, James Shields

Never in one place for long, Chavez played for his eighth and ninth major-league teams in 2018, and it was Chicago that proved to be his most productive stop yet. The 35-year-old reached a career-high strikeout rate in surprising fashion: By throwing his two best pitches by whiff rate (his curveball and changeup) notably less. The resulting three-headed fastball attack saw Chavez throw more pitches in the zone, while seeing less contact than he had previously in his career. And while that was a previously unseen approach from Chavez, it was also very much in character for a pitcher who changes his repertoire as often as his uniform. Sadly for trivia hounds but happily for Chavez, he re-upped with Texas on a two-year deal, so team no. 10 will have to wait.

YEAR	TEAM	LVL	AGE	WHIP	ERA	DRA	WARP	MPH	FB%	WHF	CSP
2016	TOR	MLB	32	1.28	4.57	4.11	0.4	95.6	66.7	10.4	50.2
2016	LAN	MLB	32	1.40	4.21	2.87	0.6	94.9	66.7	9.7	43.1
2017	ANA	MLB	33	1.40	5.35	4.80	1.1	93.1	61	9.2	46
2018	TEX	MLB	34	1.24	3.51	3.20	1.1	94.3	69.6	11.7	53.6
2018	CHN	MLB	34	0.79	1.15	2.95	0.9	94.3	69.6	11.5	53
2019	TEX	MLB	35	1.30	4.21	4.28	0.6	92.7	64	10.1	48.6

Jesse Chavez, continued

Pitch Shape vs LHH

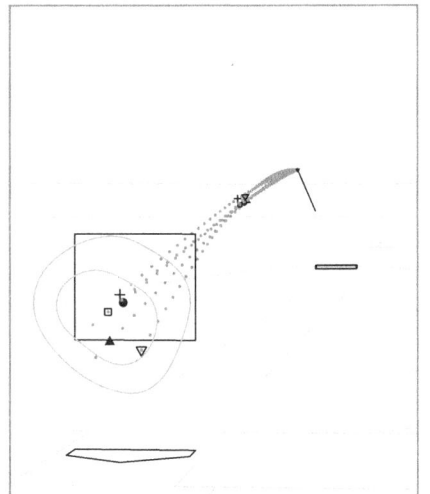

Pitch Shape vs RHH

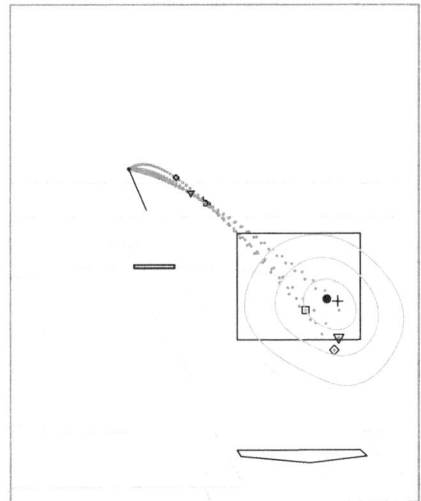

Type	Frequency	Velocity	H Movement	V Movement
● Fastball	13.7%	93.2 [102]	-7.9 [94]	-13.8 [106]
□ Sinker	28.2%	93.5 [105]	-14.2 [87]	-19.1 [104]
+ Cutter	37.0%	91.8 [118]	-2.1 [77]	-16.1 [131]
▲ Changeup	6.4%	87.2 [107]	-13.9 [86]	-28.9 [95]
× Splitter				
▽ Slider	11.8%	85.6 [105]	4.1 [97]	-32.5 [102]
◇ Curveball	2.8%	79.2 [103]	10.9 [113]	-48.1 [100]
⊕ Slow Curveball				
✳ Knuckleball				
▼ Screwball				

Taylor Guerrieri RHP

Born: 12/01/92 Age: 26 Bats: R Throws: R
Height: 6'2" Weight: 210 Origin: Round 1, 2011 Draft (#24 overall)

YEAR	TEAM	LVL	AGE	W	L	SV	G	GS	IP	H	HR	BB/9	K/9	K	GB%	BABIP
2016	MNT	AA	23	12	6	1	28	26	146	130	11	2.8	5.5	89	58%	.266
2017	DUR	AAA	24	1	0	0	2	2	9^1	7	0	1.9	11.6	12	71%	.292
2018	BUF	AAA	25	2	2	0	23	7	57^1	68	8	3.5	6.4	41	56%	.326
2018	TOR	MLB	25	0	0	0	9	0	9^2	9	1	3.7	7.4	8	59%	.286
2019	TEX	MLB	26	3	3	0	17	9	50	50	6	3.6	7.1	40	52%	.295

Breakout: 15% Improve: 21% Collapse: 13% Attrition: 25% MLB: 38%
Comparables: Myles Jaye, Jason Hursh, Zeke Spruill

Guerrieri spun 24 curveballs against major-league batters in 2018, each with the same unusual grip: right index finger crossed over the middle digit, like a wish for good luck or a white lie, and pressed along the ridge of the seams. The Blue Jays crossed their fingers just as hard for the rookie's first tryout in the big leagues, but to no avail: a squirm-inducing ERA and undisclosed health issues rushed the former top prospect right back into obscurity—and free agency.

YEAR	TEAM	LVL	AGE	WHIP	ERA	DRA	WARP	MPH	FB%	WHF	CSP
2016	MNT	AA	23	1.21	3.76	6.06	-1.7				
2017	DUR	AAA	24	0.96	2.89	1.96	0.4				
2018	BUF	AAA	25	1.57	5.18	4.27	0.7				
2018	TOR	MLB	25	1.34	4.66	4.92	0.0	93.3	76.7	12.8	42.3
2019	TEX	MLB	26	1.40	4.79	4.75	0.4	92.9	78.1	13	43.1

Taylor Guerrieri, continued

Pitch Shape vs LHH
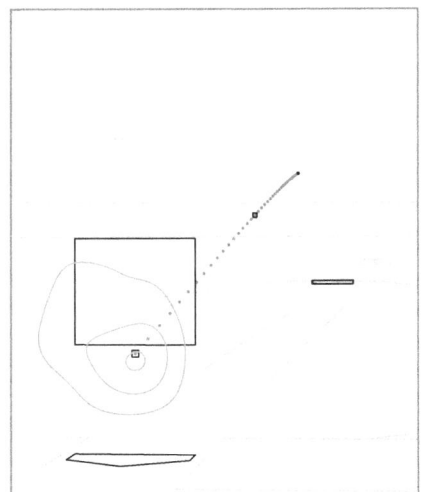

Pitch Shape vs RHH
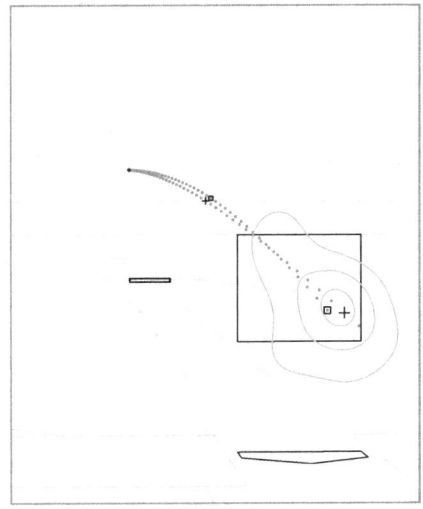

Type	Frequency	Velocity	H Movement	V Movement
● Fastball	0.6%	92.5 [100]	-13.3 [70]	-17.4 [95]
☐ Sinker	46.5%	92.6 [100]	-15.1 [79]	-22.3 [94]
+ Cutter	29.7%	91.5 [116]	-1.2 [82]	-21.2 [110]
▲ Changeup	9.3%	85.8 [102]	-16.2 [74]	-29.2 [95]
✕ Splitter				
▽ Slider				
◇ Curveball	14.0%	79.5 [104]	13.2 [122]	-54.8 [85]
✦ Slow Curveball				
✳ Knuckleball				
▼ Screwball				

Jason Hammel RHP

Born: 09/02/82   Age: 36   Bats: R   Throws: R
Height: 6'6"   Weight: 225   Origin: Round 10, 2002 Draft (#284 overall)

YEAR	TEAM	LVL	AGE	W	L	SV	G	GS	IP	H	HR	BB/9	K/9	K	GB%	BABIP
2016	CHN	MLB	33	15	10	0	30	30	166^2	148	25	2.9	7.8	144	44%	.267
2017	KCA	MLB	34	8	13	0	32	32	180^1	209	26	2.4	7.2	145	38%	.318
2018	KCA	MLB	35	4	14	0	39	18	127	168	18	2.8	6.5	92	38%	.349
2019	*TEX*	*MLB*	*36*	*1*	*1*	*0*	*3*	*3*	*15*	*17*	*3*	*3.2*	*6.6*	*11*	*40%*	*.295*

Breakout: 23%   Improve: 47%   Collapse: 13%   Attrition: 10%   MLB: 78%
Comparables: John Lackey, James Shields, Dan Haren

There's a certain art in being able to ride the wave of just-good-enough to a thirteen-year career, and Hammel has been the Picasso of this particular metier. Or perhaps Thomas Kinkade offers a better analogy, as even Hammel's best moments evoke nothing particularly interesting, bold, or memorable. In Kansas City over the past two seasons, the brushwork has become a bit sloppy, and Hammel has morphed from paint-by-numbers rotation filler to full-fledged disaster artist. The Royals, whose tolerance of bad art has been too generous at times, played the role of mean critic and declined their side of a mutual option for 2019.

YEAR	TEAM	LVL	AGE	WHIP	ERA	DRA	WARP	MPH	FB%	WHF	CSP
2016	CHN	MLB	33	1.21	3.83	4.51	1.6	94.3	51.8	10.9	46.7
2017	KCA	MLB	34	1.43	5.29	5.57	0.0	93.5	50	10.4	47.9
2018	KCA	MLB	35	1.63	6.02	6.22	-1.4	94.0	51.6	10.1	48.9
2019	*TEX*	*MLB*	*36*	*1.51*	*5.47*	*5.62*	*0.0*	*92.6*	*50*	*10.2*	*47*

Jason Hammel, continued

Pitch Shape vs LHH

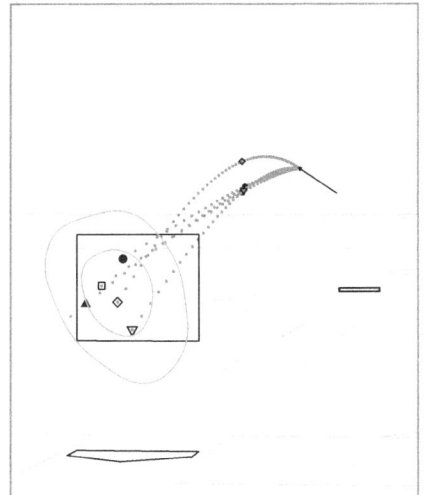

Pitch Shape vs RHH

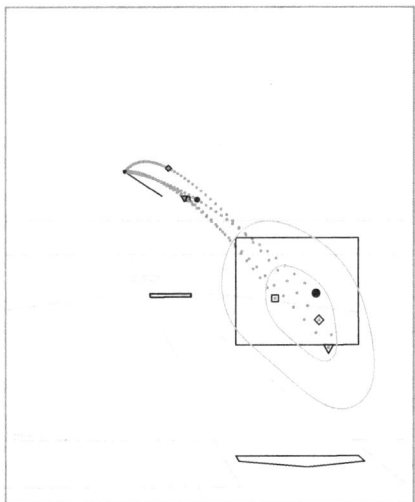

Type	Frequency	Velocity	H Movement	V Movement
● Fastball	13.7%	92.6 [100]	-6.8 [100]	-14.8 [103]
☐ Sinker	37.9%	92.2 [99]	-12.4 [102]	-18.3 [107]
+ Cutter				
▲ Changeup	4.1%	85.3 [100]	-12.1 [96]	-25.2 [106]
✕ Splitter				
▽ Slider	37.7%	85.6 [105]	5 [101]	-31.9 [103]
◇ Curveball	6.6%	77.4 [96]	11.3 [114]	-51.1 [93]
⊕ Slow Curveball				
✻ Knuckleball				
▼ Screwball				

Ariel Jurado RHP

Born: 01/30/96 Age: 23 Bats: R Throws: R
Height: 6'1" Weight: 180 Origin: International Free Agent, 2002

YEAR	TEAM	LVL	AGE	W	L	SV	G	GS	IP	H	HR	BB/9	K/9	K	GB%	BABIP
2016	HDS	A+	20	7	2	0	16	16	79^1	83	4	2.7	8.1	71	64%	.342
2016	FRI	AA	20	1	4	0	8	6	43^2	44	3	2.1	7.2	35	53%	.315
2017	FRI	AA	21	9	11	0	27	27	157	188	16	2.1	5.4	95	53%	.335
2018	FRI	AA	22	5	3	0	16	16	101^2	107	12	1.5	5.1	58	51%	.291
2018	TEX	MLB	22	5	5	0	12	8	54^2	66	7	3.0	3.6	22	52%	.304
2019	TEX	MLB	23	4	6	0	38	11	86	99	13	3.0	5.5	53	50%	.301

Breakout: 5% Improve: 12% Collapse: 19% Attrition: 24% MLB: 39%
Comparables: Zach Eflin, Michael Bowden, Dillon Gee

Jurado spent his time in the majors vacillating between looking like a young phenom on the verge of figuring it out and looking like a young man falling off that verge, not flying, and hitting every tree limb and rock on the way down. On one hand, he was 22 years old, and it frequently takes a few crash-and-burns before players catch their stride. On the other, it usually takes more than one wing to fly successfully, and Jurado's sinker has thus far been the only weapon that looks ready. When it's good, though, it's great. If he can improve his secondaries, he should be okay. If not, the bullpen awaits. You can get by with one wing in the bullpen if it's a really good wing.

YEAR	TEAM	LVL	AGE	WHIP	ERA	DRA	WARP	MPH	FB%	WHF	CSP
2016	HDS	A+	20	1.35	3.86	3.55	1.7				
2016	FRI	AA	20	1.24	3.30	3.45	0.8				
2017	FRI	AA	21	1.43	4.59	4.20	1.8				
2018	FRI	AA	22	1.22	3.28	6.18	-1.0				
2018	TEX	MLB	22	1.54	5.93	6.97	-1.1	93.3	70.2	4.8	51.2
2019	TEX	MLB	23	1.48	5.29	5.26	0.1	93.2	72.8	5	53

Ariel Jurado, continued

Pitch Shape vs LHH

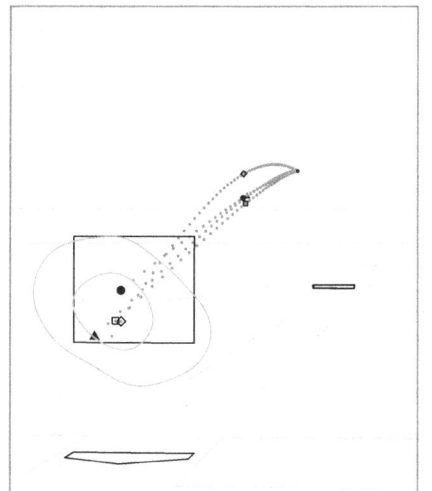

Pitch Shape vs RHH

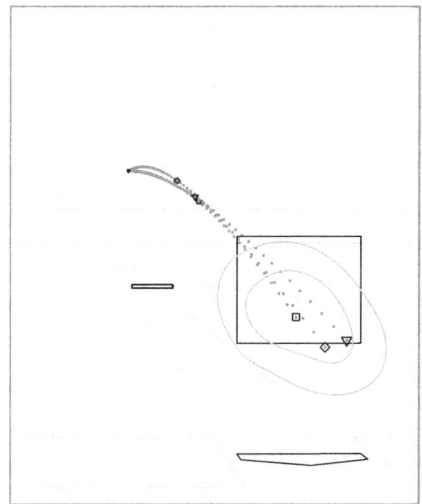

Type	Frequency	Velocity	H Movement	V Movement
● Fastball	14.3%	92.7 [101]	-7.9 [94]	-15.7 [100]
☐ Sinker	56.0%	92.2 [98]	-13.7 [91]	-21.7 [95]
+ Cutter				
▲ Changeup	11.5%	84.8 [98]	-12.4 [94]	-26.8 [102]
✕ Splitter				
▽ Slider	8.9%	85.4 [104]	2.1 [88]	-30.8 [106]
◇ Curveball	9.4%	78.9 [102]	6 [92]	-45.2 [106]
✦ Slow Curveball				
✳ Knuckleball				
▼ Screwball				

Shawn Kelley   RHP
Born: 04/26/84   Age: 35   Bats: R   Throws: R
Height: 6'2"   Weight: 237   Origin: Round 13, 2007 Draft (#405 overall)

YEAR	TEAM	LVL	AGE	W	L	SV	G	GS	IP	H	HR	BB/9	K/9	K	GB%	BABIP
2016	WAS	MLB	32	3	2	7	67	0	58	41	9	1.7	12.4	80	37%	.258
2017	WAS	MLB	33	3	2	4	33	0	26	29	12	3.8	8.7	25	26%	.236
2018	WAS	MLB	34	1	0	0	35	0	32^1	26	7	1.4	8.9	32	28%	.229
2018	OAK	MLB	34	1	0	0	19	0	16^2	7	0	3.2	9.7	18	40%	.184
2019	TEX	MLB	35	2	3	4	49	0	51	52	12	3.6	9.2	52	35%	.289

Breakout: 21%   Improve: 42%   Collapse: 27%   Attrition: 7%   MLB: 87%
Comparables: Todd Worrell, Bill Henry, Dan Miceli

Kelley was having a solid season in middle relief for Washington when Dave Martinez put him in for the ninth inning of a game the team led 25-1 over the Mets. An Austin Jackson two-run homer led to a glove slam and a look into the Nats' dugout, which in turn led to a designation for assignment, a very good 16 innings with the A's and his third postseason game pitched. That Kelley got cut for getting mad after he did a bad thing (and for *maybe* aiming some frustration at his manager, something he denied and that Martinez, at least publicly, said he did not take as showing him up) remains bizarre in a place of employment that features Angry Dudes on a daily basis. That the A's were the ones to jump in and extract value from a guy another team was unreasonably down on is enough to give you nostalgia. Remember when Billy Beane pulled off that kind of thing on a weekly basis? In any event, Kelley's a 35-year-old, two-pitch, fly-ball righty who's lost a mile and a half off his fastball over the last two years, so getting into a pissing match with Mike Rizzo might have been his last hurrah. At least he didn't go out with a whimper.

YEAR	TEAM	LVL	AGE	WHIP	ERA	DRA	WARP	MPH	FB%	WHF	CSP
2016	WAS	MLB	32	0.90	2.64	2.30	1.8	95.2	56.2	17.1	51.2
2017	WAS	MLB	33	1.54	7.27	6.11	-0.3	93.9	59.2	15.4	46.9
2018	WAS	MLB	34	0.96	3.34	4.51	0.2	93.9	52.8	12.4	50.7
2018	OAK	MLB	34	0.78	2.16	3.22	0.3	92.7	50.6	12.4	50.1
2019	TEX	MLB	35	1.40	5.81	5.55	-0.2	92.9	54.1	14.4	48.6

Shawn Kelley, continued

Pitch Shape vs LHH

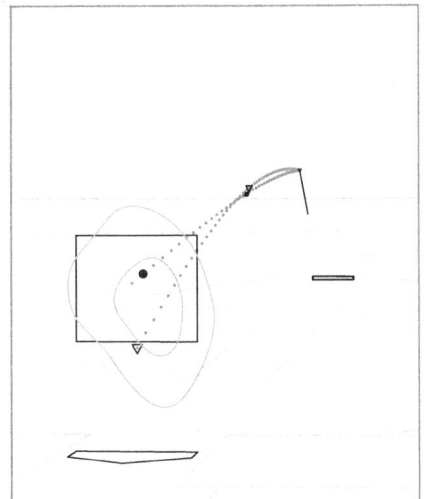

Pitch Shape vs RHH

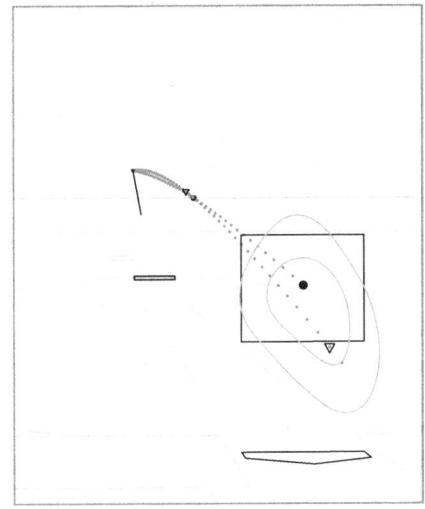

Type	Frequency	Velocity	H Movement	V Movement
● Fastball	52.1%	91.6 [97]	-1.7 [123]	-13.8 [106]
☐ Sinker				
+ Cutter				
▲ Changeup				
✕ Splitter				
▽ Slider	47.9%	81.4 [86]	5.7 [103]	-35.8 [92]
◇ Curveball				
⊕ Slow Curveball				
✴ Knuckleball				
▼ Screwball				

Jose Leclerc RHP

Born: 12/19/93   Age: 25   Bats: R   Throws: R
Height: 6'0"   Weight: 190   Origin: International Free Agent, 2010

YEAR	TEAM	LVL	AGE	W	L	SV	G	GS	IP	H	HR	BB/9	K/9	K	GB%	BABIP
2016	FRI	AA	22	0	5	1	10	2	23	17	1	3.9	11.0	28	30%	.291
2016	ROU	AAA	22	2	2	1	29	0	43	23	3	5.9	10.5	50	39%	.211
2016	TEX	MLB	22	0	0	0	12	0	15	11	0	7.8	9.0	15	29%	.289
2017	TEX	MLB	23	2	3	2	47	0	45[2]	23	4	7.9	11.8	60	40%	.204
2018	TEX	MLB	24	2	3	12	59	0	57[2]	24	1	3.9	13.3	85	34%	.211
2019	TEX	MLB	25	3	3	30	54	0	57	41	5	5.3	12.2	78	37%	.281

Breakout: 28%   Improve: 48%   Collapse: 22%   Attrition: 16%   MLB: 78%
Comparables: Carl Edwards Jr., Ken Giles, Eduardo Sanchez

For the last few years, lots of Rangers pitching prospects and young big leaguers have come with a scouting report that begins, "If he can ever figure out _____, he's going to be great." The report ends a few years later with, "Yeah, he never figured out _____." Leclerc is one glaring exception: "If he can ever figure out his control, he's going to be great" became, "He figured out his control, and now he's *nasty*." Using two different changeups to go with a plus fastball, Leclerc took over at closer when Keone Kela was traded to Pittsburgh at the deadline; across 18 innings in August and September, he did not allow an earned run and struck out 29 while holding opponents to a .226 OPS. Needless to say, he converted all 12 of his save opportunities.

YEAR	TEAM	LVL	AGE	WHIP	ERA	DRA	WARP	MPH	FB%	WHF	CSP
2016	FRI	AA	22	1.17	3.52	2.51	0.6				
2016	ROU	AAA	22	1.19	2.72	2.87	1.0				
2016	TEX	MLB	22	1.60	1.80	5.66	-0.1	97.1	61.8	12.2	44.5
2017	TEX	MLB	23	1.38	3.94	4.65	0.3	97.2	50.9	16.6	39.3
2018	TEX	MLB	24	0.85	1.56	2.87	1.4	97.3	47.8	19	44.2
2019	TEX	MLB	25	1.28	3.39	3.62	1.0	97.0	51.3	17.9	43.7

Jose Leclerc, continued

Pitch Shape vs LHH

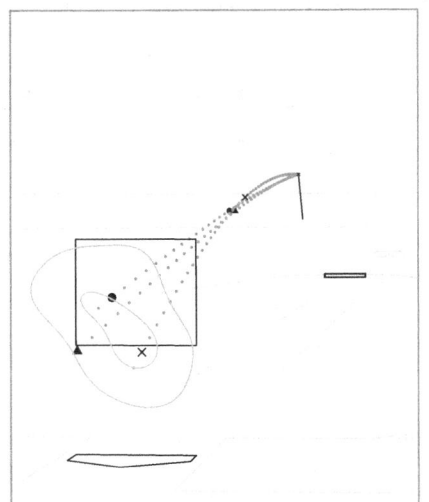

Pitch Shape vs RHH

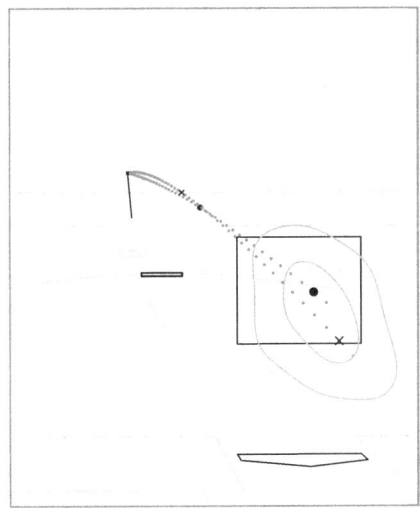

Type	Frequency	Velocity	H Movement	V Movement
● Fastball	44.3%	95.7 [110]	-2.6 [119]	-11.9 [112]
☐ Sinker	3.4%	95.6 [116]	-11.9 [106]	-19.4 [103]
+ Cutter				
▲ Changeup	6.0%	88.2 [112]	-10.6 [104]	-22.5 [114]
✕ Splitter	42.8%	81.6 [78]	9.2 [166]	-34.7 [78]
▽ Slider				
◇ Curveball	3.4%	77.6 [97]	11.5 [116]	-48.8 [98]
⊕ Slow Curveball				
✳ Knuckleball				
▼ Screwball				

Lance Lynn RHP

Born: 05/12/87 Age: 32 Bats: B Throws: R
Height: 6'5" Weight: 280 Origin: Round 1, 2008 Draft (#39 overall)

YEAR	TEAM	LVL	AGE	W	L	SV	G	GS	IP	H	HR	BB/9	K/9	K	GB%	BABIP
2017	SLN	MLB	30	11	8	0	33	33	186^1	151	27	3.8	7.4	153	45%	.244
2018	MIN	MLB	31	7	8	0	20	20	102^1	105	12	5.5	8.8	100	51%	.322
2018	NYA	MLB	31	3	2	0	11	9	54^1	58	2	2.3	10.1	61	47%	.364
2019	TEX	MLB	32	8	10	0	29	29	153^2	150	20	3.9	8.0	137	47%	.296

Breakout: 11%   Improve: 42%   Collapse: 30%   Attrition: 14%   MLB: 91%
Comparables: Doug Davis, Barry Zito, Gio Gonzalez

Originally a perceived victim of the stalled market last offseason, Lynn's $12 million deal with the Twins proved to be perfectly reasonable for his age and performance. After having an inordinately low ERA with a sky-high FIP, the real world caught up to him before he was flipped to the Yankees for Tyler Austin and Luis Rijo. Lynn posted respectable component stats for the Yankees, putting up a 2.17 FIP and a nearly five-to-one strikeout-to-walk ratio, but DRA was a bit more cynical. One could imagine him slotting into the back end of almost any rotation, which means he might be the Rangers' no. 2 after signing a three-year deal at a modest annual rate in December.

YEAR	TEAM	LVL	AGE	WHIP	ERA	DRA	WARP	MPH	FB%	WHF	CSP
2017	SLN	MLB	30	1.23	3.43	4.98	1.2	94.1	81	10.1	46
2018	MIN	MLB	31	1.63	5.10	5.53	-0.3	95.6	77	10.8	42.6
2018	NYA	MLB	31	1.33	4.14	4.32	0.6	95.4	77	11.2	46.9
2019	TEX	MLB	32	1.42	4.56	4.66	1.4	93.9	78.1	10.5	44.5

Lance Lynn, continued

Pitch Shape vs LHH

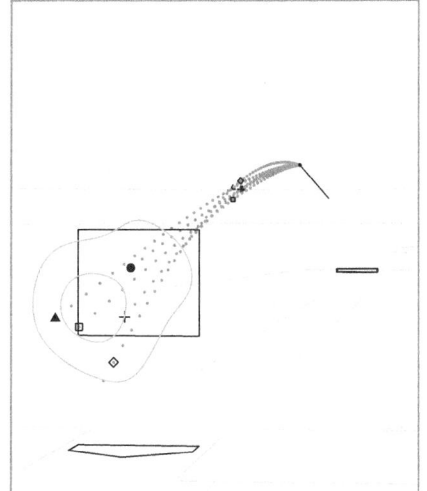

Pitch Shape vs RHH

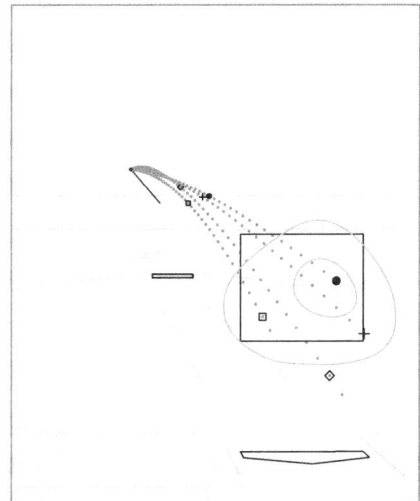

Type	Frequency	Velocity	H Movement	V Movement
● Fastball	44.8%	94.1 [105]	-4.3 [111]	-15.1 [102]
□ Sinker	32.6%	92.7 [101]	-10.4 [118]	-22.8 [92]
+ Cutter	11.3%	87.7 [93]	4.4 [114]	-28.1 [82]
▲ Changeup	2.1%	86 [103]	-9.7 [108]	-27.6 [99]
✕ Splitter				
▽ Slider				
◇ Curveball	9.1%	80.3 [107]	7.9 [100]	-47.4 [101]
⊕ Slow Curveball				
✳ Knuckleball				
▼ Screwball				

Rangers Player Analysis - 65

Chris Martin RHP

Born: 06/02/86   Age: 33   Bats: R   Throws: R
Height: 6'8"   Weight: 215   Origin: Round 21, 2005 Draft (#627 overall)

YEAR	TEAM	LVL	AGE	W	L	SV	G	GS	IP	H	HR	BB/9	K/9	K	GB%	BABIP
2018	TEX	MLB	32	1	5	0	46	0	41^2	46	5	1.1	8.0	37	41%	.323
2019	TEX	MLB	33	2	3	0	54	0	57	63	10	3.1	7.9	50	41%	.308

Breakout: 24%   Improve: 32%   Collapse: 21%   Attrition: 19%   MLB: 60%
Comparables: Randy Flores, Sam LeCure, Jean Machi

Martin came back from Japan to sign with his hometown Rangers before the 2018 season. A true feel-good story, he missed a few years with a shoulder injury, worked in a furniture warehouse, then tried out for the Grand Prairie AirHogs to kick-start his career. After time in the Red Sox organization, and in the majors with the Rockies and Yankees, Martin went to Japan and became one of the league's most dominant closers. His return stateside wasn't an overwhelming success, but it was good enough to prove that he was capable of pitching in the big leagues again.

YEAR	TEAM	LVL	AGE	WHIP	ERA	DRA	WARP	MPH	FB%	WHF	CSP
2018	TEX	MLB	32	1.22	4.54	5.29	-0.2	96.7	72.4	10.1	50.9
2019	TEX	MLB	33	1.46	5.15	4.99	0.1	95.6	71.5	10	50.3

Chris Martin, continued

Pitch Shape vs LHH

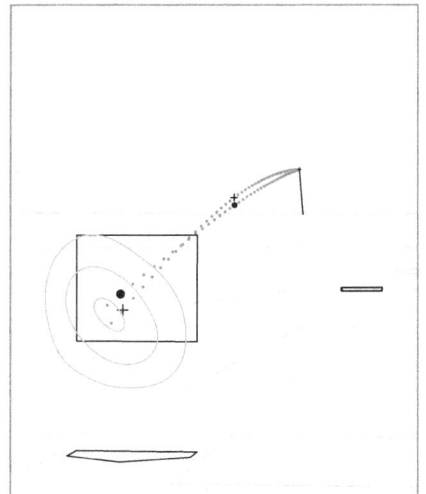

Pitch Shape vs RHH

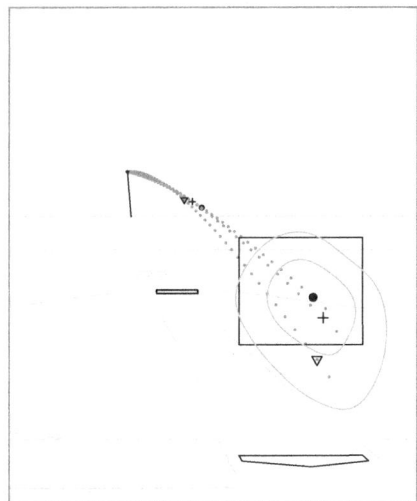

Type	Frequency	Velocity	H Movement	V Movement
● Fastball	50.4%	95.8 [110]	-4.4 [110]	-13.3 [108]
□ Sinker	0.9%	94.6 [111]	-11.8 [107]	-19.6 [102]
+ Cutter	21.2%	91.3 [115]	3.7 [110]	-23.6 [101]
▲ Changeup	5.5%	87.7 [110]	-8.4 [115]	-28.1 [98]
× Splitter				
▽ Slider	22.0%	84.8 [102]	3.7 [95]	-36.3 [90]
◇ Curveball				
⊕ Slow Curveball				
✳ Knuckleball				
▼ Screwball				

Texas Rangers 2019

Yohander Mendez LHP
Born: 01/17/95   Age: 24   Bats: L   Throws: L
Height: 6'5"   Weight: 200   Origin: International Free Agent, 2011

YEAR	TEAM	LVL	AGE	W	L	SV	G	GS	IP	H	HR	BB/9	K/9	K	GB%	BABIP
2016	HDS	A+	21	4	1	0	7	7	33	21	2	3.0	12.3	45	51%	.264
2016	FRI	AA	21	4	1	0	10	10	46²	39	2	2.7	8.9	46	47%	.296
2016	ROU	AAA	21	4	1	0	7	4	31¹	12	0	4.6	6.3	22	40%	.150
2016	TEX	MLB	21	0	0	0	2	0	3	5	0	6.0	0.0	0	33%	.333
2017	FRI	AA	22	7	8	0	24	24	137²	114	23	2.8	8.1	124	46%	.256
2017	TEX	MLB	22	0	1	0	7	0	12¹	13	3	2.2	5.1	7	37%	.263
2018	DEB	A+	23	1	2	0	5	5	31	29	3	1.7	7.8	27	36%	.306
2018	FRI	AA	23	1	1	0	6	6	33	33	6	2.7	8.7	32	32%	.300
2018	ROU	AAA	23	0	7	0	12	12	58¹	65	13	3.7	7.7	50	40%	.310
2018	TEX	MLB	23	2	2	0	8	5	27²	28	4	4.9	5.9	18	40%	.286
2019	TEX	MLB	24	2	3	0	8	8	40	41	7	3.7	7.5	33	41%	.291

Breakout: 12%   Improve: 29%   Collapse: 30%   Attrition: 39%   MLB: 71%
Comparables: Anthony Bass, Jake Odorizzi, Aaron Blair

Mendez is the latest success story for Roy Silver, the Josh Hamilton and Matt Bush whisperer. The tall southpaw was part of a group of players who violated team rules in Kansas City in June, and he found himself in High-A after landing on that really long slide in Chutes and Ladders. Mendez worked his way back through the minor leagues and was — save for one bad start against the Rays — markedly better after his return to Arlington in September.

YEAR	TEAM	LVL	AGE	WHIP	ERA	DRA	WARP	MPH	FB%	WHF	CSP
2016	HDS	A+	21	0.97	2.45	2.13	1.3				
2016	FRI	AA	21	1.14	3.09	3.53	0.9				
2016	ROU	AAA	21	0.89	0.57	4.23	0.3				
2016	TEX	MLB	21	2.33	18.00	4.29	0.0	95.0	48	12.3	41.1
2017	FRI	AA	22	1.14	3.79	3.24	3.2				
2017	TEX	MLB	22	1.30	5.11	7.67	-0.3	94.1	60.7	10	46.7
2018	DEB	A+	23	1.13	3.48	3.93	0.5				
2018	FRI	AA	23	1.30	4.91	5.08	0.1				
2018	ROU	AAA	23	1.53	5.25	4.39	0.8				
2018	TEX	MLB	23	1.55	5.53	7.02	-0.6	94.2	59.9	9.6	48.3
2019	TEX	MLB	24	1.41	5.20	5.34	0.0	94.0	61.1	10.1	47.3

Yohander Mendez, continued

Pitch Shape vs LHH

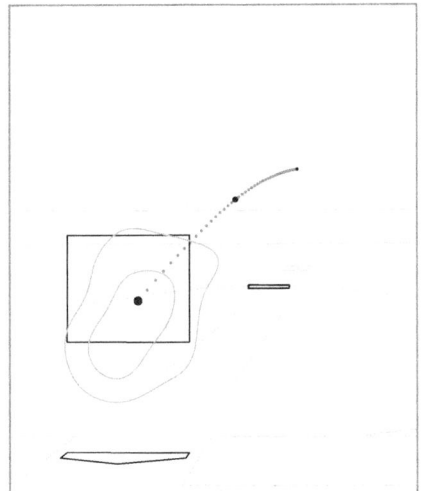

Pitch Shape vs RHH

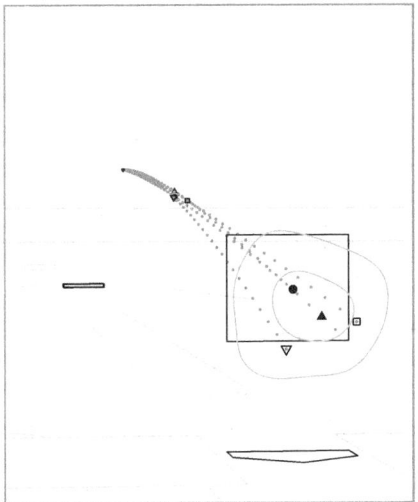

Type		Frequency	Velocity	H Movement	V Movement
●	Fastball	47.5%	92.5 [100]	7.6 [96]	-15.8 [100]
□	Sinker	12.4%	91.1 [93]	14.2 [87]	-21 [98]
+	Cutter				
▲	Changeup	22.2%	83.2 [92]	10.9 [102]	-27.5 [100]
×	Splitter				
▽	Slider	12.8%	84.4 [100]	-2.1 [88]	-28.9 [112]
◇	Curveball	5.1%	79.1 [102]	-4.8 [87]	-39.1 [120]
✥	Slow Curveball				
✶	Knuckleball				
▼	Screwball				

Rangers Player Analysis - 69

Shelby Miller RHP

Born: 10/10/90   Age: 28   Bats: R   Throws: R
Height: 6'3"   Weight: 225   Origin: Round 1, 2009 Draft (#19 overall)

YEAR	TEAM	LVL	AGE	W	L	SV	G	GS	IP	H	HR	BB/9	K/9	K	GB%	BABIP
2016	VIS	A+	25	2	0	0	2	2	12	8	0	0.8	14.2	19	46%	.308
2016	RNO	AAA	25	5	1	0	8	8	50^2	55	4	1.8	9.8	55	52%	.367
2016	ARI	MLB	25	3	12	0	20	20	101	127	14	3.7	6.2	70	44%	.340
2017	ARI	MLB	26	2	2	0	4	4	22	20	1	4.9	8.2	20	46%	.288
2018	VIS	A+	27	1	0	0	2	2	11^2	7	0	0.0	13.9	18	46%	.292
2018	ARI	MLB	27	0	4	0	5	4	16	24	5	4.5	10.7	19	52%	.404
2019	TEX	MLB	28	5	6	0	18	18	90	85	10	3.9	8.7	87	44%	.297

Breakout: 14%   Improve: 52%   Collapse: 21%   Attrition: 13%   MLB: 91%
Comparables: Chris Tillman, Noah Lowry, Homer Bailey

When Arizona traded no. 1 overall pick Dansby Swanson and Ender Inciarte to the Braves for Miller, most said the trade was terrible. In hindsight, though, it was worse than that. Miller returned from elbow surgery in 2018 and pitched erratically. His velocity was fine and he got his strikeouts, but he couldn't reliably command his stuff and allowed too many home runs in too few innings. Absolutely no one knows what to expect of him in the future. Starter? Reliever? Retiree? Three years of injuries and poor results make his 2015 excellence a thing of the past and the Diamondbacks are left holding the bag. Somewhere, Dave Stewart is ordering another Mai Tai. Or maybe a few if Swanson ever lives up to his hype.

YEAR	TEAM	LVL	AGE	WHIP	ERA	DRA	WARP	MPH	FB%	WHF	CSP
2016	VIS	A+	25	0.75	0.75	3.78	0.2				
2016	RNO	AAA	25	1.28	3.91	4.62	0.4				
2016	ARI	MLB	25	1.67	6.15	7.00	-1.9	95.9	62.6	8.6	50
2017	ARI	MLB	26	1.45	4.09	4.24	0.3	97.1	58.1	10.2	51.3
2018	VIS	A+	27	0.60	0.77	3.15	0.3				
2018	ARI	MLB	27	2.00	10.69	4.22	0.2	96.4	63.7	9.4	48.6
2019	TEX	MLB	28	1.39	4.13	4.20	1.3	95.6	62.4	9.1	50.2

Shelby Miller, continued

Pitch Shape vs LHH

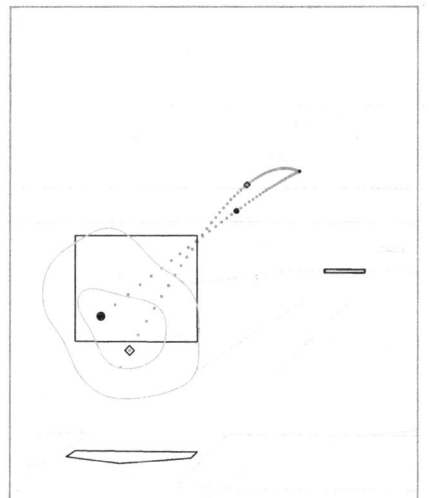

Pitch Shape vs RHH

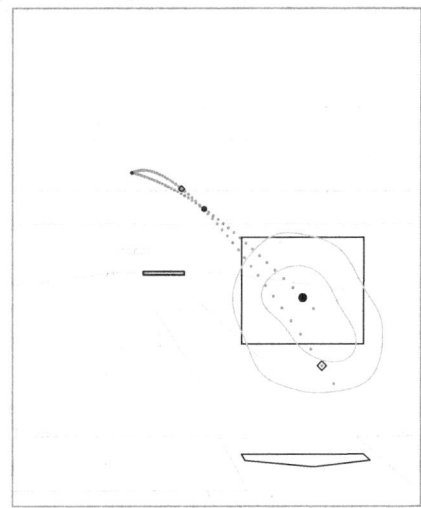

Type	Frequency	Velocity	H Movement	V Movement
● Fastball	60.1%	95 [108]	-8.4 [92]	-13.3 [108]
☐ Sinker	3.7%	93.5 [105]	-13.6 [92]	-18.3 [107]
+ Cutter	11.9%	89.9 [107]	0.6 [93]	-23.7 [100]
▲ Changeup	0.6%	88.6 [113]	-10.5 [104]	-19.4 [124]
✕ Splitter				
▽ Slider				
◇ Curveball	23.8%	80.3 [107]	5.4 [90]	-44.6 [108]
⊕ Slow Curveball				
✶ Knuckleball				
▼ Screwball				

Rangers Player Analysis - 71

Mike Minor LHP

Born: 12/26/87   Age: 31   Bats: R   Throws: L
Height: 6'4"   Weight: 210   Origin: Round 1, 2009 Draft (#7 overall)

YEAR	TEAM	LVL	AGE	W	L	SV	G	GS	IP	H	HR	BB/9	K/9	K	GB%	BABIP
2016	OMA	AAA	28	0	4	0	8	8	34^2	38	7	4.4	8.6	33	37%	.333
2017	KCA	MLB	29	6	6	6	65	0	77^2	57	5	2.5	10.2	88	43%	.272
2018	TEX	MLB	30	12	8	0	28	28	157	138	25	2.2	7.6	132	35%	.259
2019	TEX	MLB	31	8	11	0	28	28	159	163	29	3.4	7.9	140	38%	.292

Breakout: 23%   Improve: 52%   Collapse: 23%   Attrition: 19%   MLB: 91%
Comparables: Tom Gorzelanny, Brandon Morrow, Matt Garza

Minor is a case study in looking better than season totals. In his first year back in a starting role after injuries made him a reliever, it took him a couple of months to really lock it in. In April and May, opponents hit .282, sticking him with a 5.79 ERA. From June onward, however, those numbers were .204 and 3.23, a total turnaround that lasted until the Rangers shut him down in late September, citing an innings limit. Speaking of innings, he pitched 157 of them, nearly 80 more than in 2017 for Kansas City. He finished the season healthy, so maybe that number is nothing more than a shady character in the corner of the room who turns out to be harmlessly eating his lunch: Keep an eye on it, but no need to talk to the manager yet.

YEAR	TEAM	LVL	AGE	WHIP	ERA	DRA	WARP	MPH	FB%	WHF	CSP
2016	OMA	AAA	28	1.59	6.23	4.12	0.5				
2017	KCA	MLB	29	1.02	2.55	2.96	1.9	96.1	45.7	13.5	46.5
2018	TEX	MLB	30	1.12	4.18	5.78	-0.9	94.8	49.5	10.9	50.5
2019	TEX	MLB	31	1.40	5.12	5.24	0.3	94.3	48.1	11.5	48.5

Mike Minor, continued

Pitch Shape vs LHH

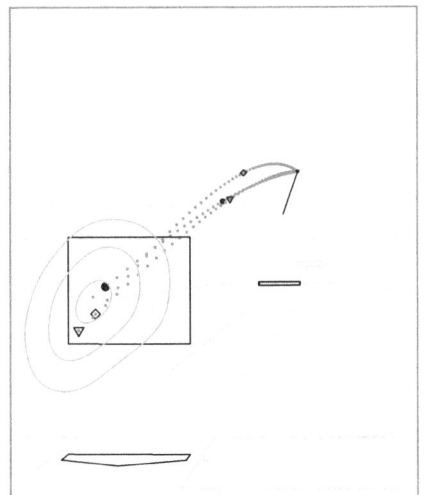

Pitch Shape vs RHH

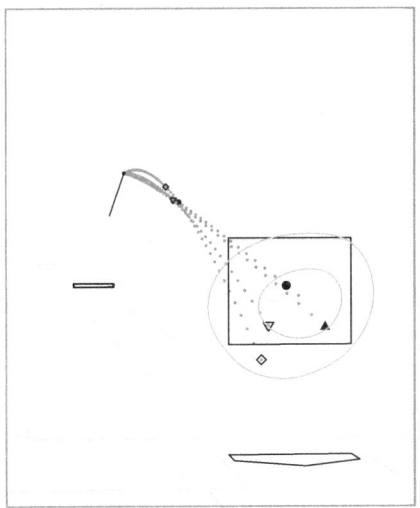

Type	Frequency	Velocity	H Movement	V Movement
● Fastball	48.5%	93.2 [102]	5.5 [105]	-13.7 [107]
☐ Sinker	1.0%	88.3 [79]	13 [97]	-19.9 [102]
+ Cutter				
▲ Changeup	18.8%	86.2 [104]	14.7 [82]	-22.7 [114]
✕ Splitter				
▽ Slider	20.9%	87.7 [115]	-3.1 [93]	-24.8 [124]
◇ Curveball	10.8%	80.9 [109]	-3.7 [83]	-44.4 [108]
⊕ Slow Curveball				
✱ Knuckleball				
▼ Screwball				

Rangers Player Analysis - 73

C.D. Pelham LHP

Born: 02/21/95   Age: 24   Bats: L   Throws: L
Height: 6'6"   Weight: 235   Origin: Round 33, 2015 Draft (#978 overall)

YEAR	TEAM	LVL	AGE	W	L	SV	G	GS	IP	H	HR	BB/9	K/9	K	GB%	BABIP
2016	SPO	A-	21	0	6	2	16	7	38	36	0	10.2	11.8	50	48%	.364
2017	HIC	A	22	4	2	13	37	0	62^1	47	6	3.8	10.8	75	46%	.266
2018	DEB	A+	23	0	0	11	23	0	27^2	23	0	4.2	11.1	34	53%	.311
2018	FRI	AA	23	2	0	2	24	0	19	20	1	6.2	9.0	19	48%	.345
2018	TEX	MLB	23	0	0	0	10	0	7^2	12	0	4.7	8.2	7	52%	.444
2019	TEX	MLB	24	1	2	0	32	0	34^1	33	5	8.6	9.2	35	42%	.302

Breakout: 1%   Improve: 2%   Collapse: 1%   Attrition: 1%   MLB: 4%
Comparables: Taylor Thompson, Ryan Burr, Jaye Chapman

Pelham is a big southpaw who throws the ball *real* hard, so we're not going to worry too much about his MLB numbers yet. Instead, let's focus on the fact that he started the season in High-A, played in the Futures Game and, after a brief pit stop in Double-A Frisco, made it to the bigs. That's a heck of a year for the South Carolina native. As he looks forward to 2019, he'll undoubtedly be hoping to cut down on walks and significantly lower his BHtAMOoTB/9 (Batters Hitting the Absolute Mess Out of the Ball per nine innings).

YEAR	TEAM	LVL	AGE	WHIP	ERA	DRA	WARP	MPH	FB%	WHF	CSP
2016	SPO	A-	21	2.08	6.16	3.21	0.8				
2017	HIC	A	22	1.17	3.18	2.78	1.5				
2018	DEB	A+	23	1.30	1.95	3.04	0.6				
2018	FRI	AA	23	1.74	6.16	4.66	0.1				
2018	TEX	MLB	23	2.09	7.04	7.47	-0.2	98.4	77.1	8.9	51.2
2019	TEX	MLB	24	1.96	6.77	6.49	-0.5	98.2	79.4	9.2	52.7

C.D. Pelham, continued

Pitch Shape vs LHH

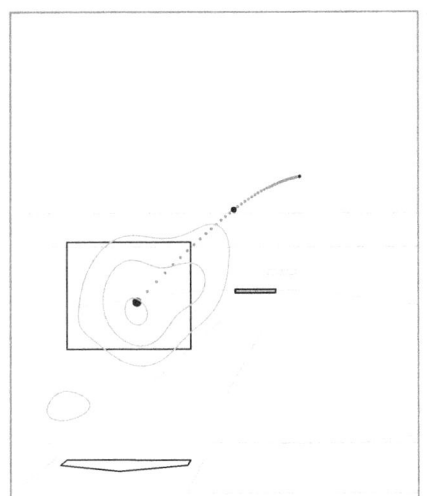

Pitch Shape vs RHH

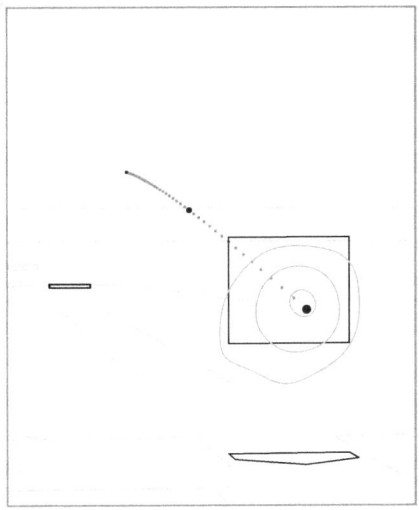

Type	Frequency	Velocity	H Movement	V Movement
● Fastball	77.1%	96.9 [114]	5.8 [104]	-14.7 [103]
☐ Sinker				
+ Cutter				
▲ Changeup	2.5%	85.1 [99]	11.9 [97]	-24.8 [108]
✕ Splitter				
▽ Slider	20.4%	84.3 [99]	-5.4 [102]	-35 [94]
◇ Curveball				
⊕ Slow Curveball				
✶ Knuckleball				
▼ Screwball				

Adrian Sampson   RHP

Born: 10/07/91   Age: 27   Bats: R   Throws: R
Height: 6'2"   Weight: 210   Origin: Round 5, 2012 Draft (#166 overall)

YEAR	TEAM	LVL	AGE	W	L	SV	G	GS	IP	H	HR	BB/9	K/9	K	GB%	BABIP
2016	TAC	AAA	24	7	4	0	13	13	80^1	81	5	1.3	6.8	61	49%	.310
2016	SEA	MLB	24	0	1	0	1	1	4^2	8	2	1.9	3.9	2	33%	.375
2017	RNG	RK	25	1	1	0	4	4	12^2	11	0	0.7	5.0	7	56%	.282
2017	DEB	A+	25	0	1	0	2	2	8^2	13	1	1.0	7.3	7	55%	.375
2017	ROU	AAA	25	1	0	0	2	2	10	10	0	0.9	6.3	7	39%	.323
2018	ROU	AAA	26	8	4	0	33	19	126^2	137	12	1.7	6.0	85	44%	.304
2018	TEX	MLB	26	0	3	0	5	4	23	24	6	1.6	5.9	15	39%	.261
2019	TEX	MLB	27	5	8	0	19	19	105	121	19	2.9	6.2	73	44%	.301

Breakout: 2%   Improve: 7%   Collapse: 18%   Attrition: 24%   MLB: 36%
Comparables: Zachary Neal, Eric Jokisch, Brady Rodgers

In late 2016, the Seattle native injured his right elbow while throwing warm-up pitches before his first big-league start for the Mariners. The injury cost him nearly two years, before he finally cracked the big leagues with Texas in September. He made four starts, the last of which came in Seattle during the last week of the season. After the game, about 60 of Sampson's friends and relatives were allowed to wait outside the clubhouse for him. He emerged to a loud echo of cheers and applause as smiles and tears abounded. There's no clever joke here for Sampson, that's just a fun story to tell.

YEAR	TEAM	LVL	AGE	WHIP	ERA	DRA	WARP	MPH	FB%	WHF	CSP
2016	TAC	AAA	24	1.16	3.25	3.12	2.0				
2016	SEA	MLB	24	1.93	7.71	9.16	-0.2	94.4	68.2	3.5	52
2017	RNG	RK	25	0.95	4.26	5.46	0.1				
2017	DEB	A+	25	1.62	5.19	3.76	0.2				
2017	ROU	AAA	25	1.10	0.90	3.58	0.2				
2018	ROU	AAA	26	1.27	3.77	4.06	2.0				
2018	TEX	MLB	26	1.22	4.30	6.43	-0.3	92.5	57.5	8.3	45.3
2019	TEX	MLB	27	1.47	5.57	5.57	-0.1	92.2	59.6	7.7	48.4

Adrian Sampson, continued

Pitch Shape vs LHH

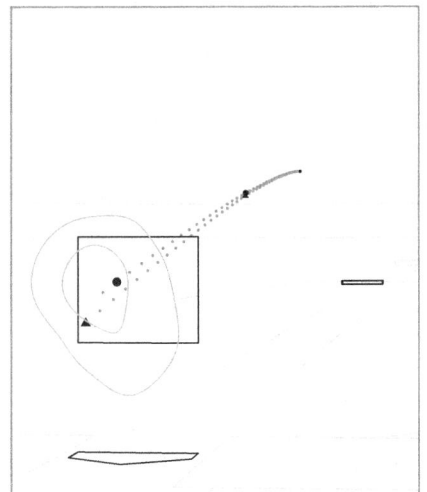

Pitch Shape vs RHH

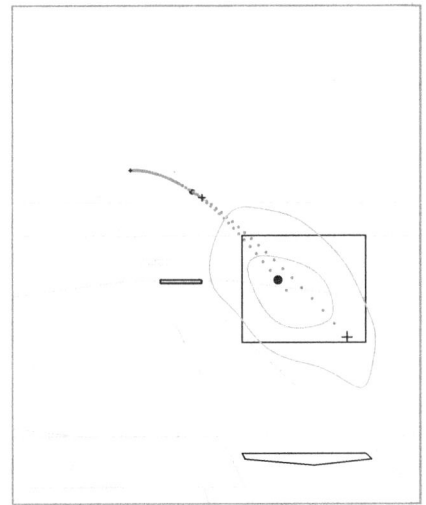

Type	Frequency	Velocity	H Movement	V Movement
● Fastball	57.5%	91.5 [97]	-11.7 [77]	-19.3 [89]
☐ Sinker				
+ Cutter	15.6%	87.2 [91]	-1 [83]	-30.1 [74]
▲ Changeup	22.1%	86.4 [104]	-14.6 [82]	-25 [107]
× Splitter				
▽ Slider	4.7%	83 [94]	3.1 [92]	-36.9 [88]
◇ Curveball				
⊕ Slow Curveball				
✳ Knuckleball				
▼ Screwball				

Jeffrey Springs LHP
Born: 09/20/92 Age: 26 Bats: L Throws: L
Height: 6'3" Weight: 180 Origin: Round 30, 2015 Draft (#888 overall)

YEAR	TEAM	LVL	AGE	W	L	SV	G	GS	IP	H	HR	BB/9	K/9	K	GB%	BABIP
2016	HIC	A	23	1	1	3	18	0	31	11	1	2.3	11.6	40	57%	.156
2016	HDS	A+	23	2	2	0	13	9	48²	52	9	3.9	9.6	52	44%	.321
2017	DEB	A+	24	2	8	2	31	17	112¹	104	13	3.0	11.7	146	36%	.336
2018	FRI	AA	25	3	2	1	20	0	37¹	39	2	1.7	16.4	68	41%	.487
2018	ROU	AAA	25	1	2	1	13	0	19¹	12	0	5.6	14.0	30	44%	.333
2018	TEX	MLB	25	1	1	0	18	2	32	32	4	3.9	8.7	31	33%	.308
2019	*TEX*	*MLB*	*26*	*2*	*3*	*0*	*54*	*0*	*57*	*52*	*8*	*4.0*	*10.5*	*67*	*39%*	*.303*

Breakout: 22% Improve: 34% Collapse: 12% Attrition: 24% MLB: 50%
Comparables: Andrew Brown, Bobby Wahl, Spencer Patton

When the Rangers became the latest team to employ an "opener," Springs was the man. The rookie pitched well for the Rangers in his inaugural campaign, both early and late in games. He did continue his trend from the minor leagues of stringing together a handful of very impressive outings, only to level his stats all at once with a belly-flop. His ERA was still 3.38, but take away those three bad outings and it plummets to 0.91 (that sample includes 29 2/3 of his 32 innings). Of course, you can be that selective only when you have a narrative to push, so instead, let's just agree that he'll have a shot to break camp with the big kids in 2019.

YEAR	TEAM	LVL	AGE	WHIP	ERA	DRA	WARP	MPH	FB%	WHF	CSP
2016	HIC	A	23	0.61	1.16	2.24	0.9				
2016	HDS	A+	23	1.50	5.36	5.91	-0.3				
2017	DEB	A+	24	1.26	3.69	2.66	3.3				
2018	FRI	AA	25	1.23	4.82	2.00	1.3				
2018	ROU	AAA	25	1.24	2.79	1.87	0.7				
2018	TEX	MLB	25	1.44	3.38	5.95	-0.4	92.9	62.8	11.9	52.4
2019	*TEX*	*MLB*	*26*	*1.37*	*4.23*	*4.30*	*0.6*	*92.5*	*63.9*	*12.2*	*53.3*

Jeffrey Springs, continued

Pitch Shape vs LHH

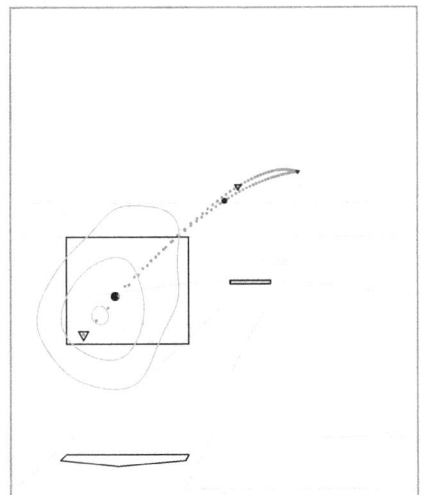

Pitch Shape vs RHH

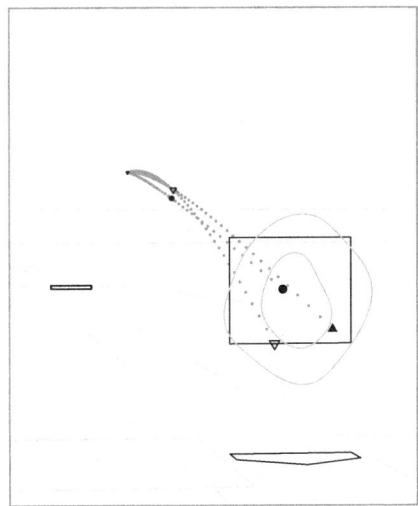

Type	Frequency	Velocity	H Movement	V Movement
● Fastball	57.0%	91.9 [98]	11.3 [79]	-16.1 [99]
☐ Sinker	5.7%	91.3 [94]	14.5 [84]	-19.8 [102]
+ Cutter				
▲ Changeup	23.2%	79.6 [77]	9.2 [111]	-27.9 [98]
× Splitter				
▽ Slider	14.1%	82.2 [90]	-3.7 [95]	-37.1 [88]
◇ Curveball				
✥ Slow Curveball				
✱ Knuckleball				
▼ Screwball				

Jett Bandy C

Born: 03/26/90 Age: 29 Bats: R Throws: R
Height: 6'4" Weight: 235 Origin: Round 31, 2011 Draft (#945 overall)

YEAR	TEAM	LVL	AGE	PA	R	2B	3B	HR	RBI	BB	K	SB	CS	AVG/OBP/SLG
2016	SLC	AAA	26	105	13	7	0	2	21	2	19	2	1	.274/.314/.411
2016	ANA	MLB	26	231	23	9	0	8	25	11	38	1	0	.234/.281/.392
2017	CSP	AAA	27	51	7	2	0	2	14	5	5	0	1	.310/.412/.500
2017	MIL	MLB	27	188	14	6	0	6	18	15	51	1	0	.207/.287/.349
2018	MIL	MLB	28	71	5	2	0	1	1	3	23	0	0	.188/.268/.266
2018	CSP	AAA	28	216	23	15	0	9	35	10	32	3	0	.292/.353/.510
2019	TEX	MLB	29	35	4	2	0	1	4	2	8	0	0	.250/.314/.406

Breakout: 9% Improve: 36% Collapse: 9% Attrition: 27% MLB: 68%
Comparables: Carlos Ruiz, Josh Phegley, Landon Powell

Even though the surface stats in the majors suggest the dream ended for Bandy in 2018, the depth catcher made things interesting at Triple-A Colorado Springs. Bandy raked for the Sky Sox, even with the inflated offensive environment taken into consideration, and established himself as a Quad-A player who might get another MLB shot in a catching-starved league. Indeed, Bandy's own parent club demonstrated that playable catchers can be old and still (seemingly) come out of nowhere, so it's not yet time to give up hope of a future MLB role. The problem is that even if Bandy made adjustments that help the bat play, the glove lagged behind, making it more difficult to see someone taking a chance on the overall profile.

YEAR	TEAM	P. COUNT	FRM RUNS	BLK RUNS	THRW RUNS	TOT RUNS
2016	ANA	8749	-1.0	1.5	1.9	1.7
2017	CSP	1201	-1.0	-0.3	0.0	-1.0
2017	MIL	6970	-2.4	-0.8	-0.8	-4.6
2018	CSP	4214	-0.9	0.0	0.1	-0.8
2018	MIL	2860	-0.6	-0.5	0.1	-1.2
2019	TEX	1347	-0.5	0.0	0.0	-0.5

YEAR	TEAM	LVL	AGE	PA	DRC+	VORP	BABIP	BRR	FRAA	WARP
2016	SLC	AAA	26	105	77	1.8	.312	-2.7	C(21): 1.2	-0.1
2016	ANA	MLB	26	231	99	4.2	.246	-2.0	C(68): 2.7	1.2
2017	CSP	AAA	27	51	120	1.8	.306	-0.6	C(9): -1.5	0.1
2017	MIL	MLB	27	188	77	0.1	.259	-1.9	C(50): -3.4	-0.1
2018	MIL	MLB	28	71	63	-0.5	.275	0.1	C(22): -1.3	-0.1
2018	CSP	AAA	28	216	119	13.0	.305	-0.4	C(29): -1.0, 1B(21): -1.9	0.6
2019	TEX	MLB	29	35	96	1.3	.287	0.0	C -1	0.1

Pedro Gonzalez CF

Born: 10/27/97 Age: 21 Bats: R Throws: R
Height: 6'5" Weight: 190 Origin: International Free Agent, 2014

YEAR	TEAM	LVL	AGE	PA	R	2B	3B	HR	RBI	BB	K	SB	CS	AVG/OBP/SLG
2016	DRO	RK	18	30	3	0	1	0	6	2	4	4	1	.222/.300/.296
2016	GJR	RK	18	248	32	15	8	2	19	14	77	6	7	.230/.290/.394
2017	GJR	RK	19	209	28	16	6	3	28	18	53	11	6	.321/.388/.519
2018	HIC	A	20	371	47	17	5	12	46	28	110	9	5	.234/.296/.421
2019	TEX	MLB	21	251	22	7	1	6	20	6	88	2	1	.151/.170/.270

Breakout: 0% Improve: 1% Collapse: 0% Attrition: 1% MLB: 1%
Comparables: Teoscar Hernandez, Keon Broxton, Daniel Fields

Far be it from the fine folks at BP to believe in curses, but hear us out: Since the Rangers lost Game 6 of the 2011 World Series, their first-round picks have been cursed. Consider: Lewis Brinson in 2012 and Luis Ortiz in 2014. (Chi Chi Gonzalez and Travis Demeritte were the picks in 2013, and Dillon Tate — shipped to the Yankees for a couple months' worth of Carlos Beltran in 2016 — was their 2015 selection, if you need additional context.) Not only have none of them become above-replacement big leaguers, but after Ortiz and Brinson were packaged together and sent to Milwaukee in 2016 for Jonathan Lucroy and Jeremy Jeffress, both returning players became markedly worse versions of themselves upon arrival, suggesting that the curse is transferable. Lucroy was sent to Colorado in 2017 for this Gonzalez, who showed flashes of greatness in Spokane and fall instructs, but struggled mightily in Low-A Hickory for the entirety of the 2018 season.

To break the curse, Texas needs a few things to happen. First, Gonzalez needs a big 2019 season. Next, Tayler Scott (the return for Jeffress) must become the first South African pitcher to make it to the big leagues. And lastly, David Freese must donate one-third of his bones to be ground into a paste and thrown into a volcano. Alternatively, one of Ragans (2016), Bubba Thompson (2017) or Cole Winn (2018) could just be a star in Texas, and that would set everything right.

YEAR	TEAM	LVL	AGE	PA	DRC+	VORP	BABIP	BRR	FRAA	WARP
2016	DRO	RK	18	30	93	0.0	.261	-1.0	CF(7): 0.3	0.0
2016	GJR	RK	18	248	43	8.6	.336	1.8	CF(57): 2.5	-0.7
2017	GJR	RK	19	209	96	13.6	.432	0.9	CF(41): -3.9	-0.1
2018	HIC	A	20	371	92	11.7	.307	1.7	CF(60): 4.7, LF(20): -1.1	1.0
2019	TEX	MLB	21	251	7	-19.2	.201	0.1	CF 0, LF 0	-2.1

Scott Heineman OF

Born: 12/04/92 Age: 26 Bats: R Throws: R
Height: 6'1" Weight: 215 Origin: Round 11, 2015 Draft (#318 overall)

YEAR	TEAM	LVL	AGE	PA	R	2B	3B	HR	RBI	BB	K	SB	CS	AVG/OBP/SLG
2016	HDS	A+	23	610	96	39	8	17	80	59	120	30	14	.303/.386/.505
2017	FRI	AA	24	529	82	26	7	9	44	50	121	12	9	.284/.363/.427
2018	FRI	AA	25	31	6	2	0	1	10	7	5	2	1	.522/.613/.739
2018	ROU	AAA	25	469	68	20	2	11	57	32	93	16	8	.295/.355/.429
2019	TEX	MLB	26	117	14	5	1	3	13	6	29	2	1	.259/.302/.407

Breakout: 4% Improve: 23% Collapse: 9% Attrition: 25% MLB: 46%
Comparables: Lane Adams, Brian Goodwin, Johnny Field

Some minor-league coaches say you can tell which guys are going to be big leaguers just by the way they walk onto a field. One coach, when asked for an example, said: "Scott Heineman." He followed that up with, "Of course, I'm not saying he's *definitely* going to make it to the big leagues, but watch him walk." He was right — Heineman walks with an effervescent bounce that speaks volumes about his joy for the game and confidence in his abilities. The coach was probably right about him being a big leaguer as well; it would be shocking if he didn't make his debut in 2019. Frankly, it was a little surprising he didn't get a September call-up in 2018.

YEAR	TEAM	LVL	AGE	PA	DRC+	VORP	BABIP	BRR	FRAA	WARP
2016	HDS	A+	23	610	128	40.3	.360	1.2	LF(91): -3.3, CF(40): 1.3	1.7
2017	FRI	AA	24	529	113	29.5	.365	6.8	LF(72): -8.5, CF(29): -2.9	0.1
2018	FRI	AA	25	31	261	5.3	.611	-0.9	CF(5): -0.9, LF(2): 0.0	0.4
2018	ROU	AAA	25	469	111	24.6	.353	4.0	RF(48): 1.7, CF(44): -3.3	1.4
2019	TEX	MLB	26	117	94	3.3	.319	0.0	CF -1, LF 0	0.2

Julio Pablo Martinez   CF

Born: 03/21/96   Age: 23   Bats: L   Throws: L
Height: 5'9"   Weight: 174   Origin: International Free Agent, 2018

YEAR	TEAM	LVL	AGE	PA	R	2B	3B	HR	RBI	BB	K	SB	CS	AVG/OBP/SLG
2018	DRG	RK	22	33	10	1	1	1	3	9	7	2	3	.409/.606/.682
2018	SPO	A-	22	273	49	9	5	8	21	34	69	11	6	.252/.351/.436
2019	TEX	MLB	23	251	25	4	1	8	21	18	92	3	1	.124/.186/.255

Breakout: 3%   Improve: 4%   Collapse: 0%   Attrition: 4%   MLB: 4%
Comparables: Adam Engel, Blake Tekotte, Michael Taylor

The young Cuban was the Rangers' consolation prize for not winning the Shohei Ohtani sweepstakes, and after signing with Texas he utterly demolished the Dominican Summer League for seven whole games before Texas moved him to Spokane, where he was, in order, pretty okay, pretty good and then *really* good in six playoff games, hitting .348/.423/.696. He didn't let up on the gas pedal when the season ended, either, hitting .327/.397/.519 in the Arizona Fall League. He won't be in the big leagues in 2019, but when Texas is ready to contend again, there's a good chance they'll be doing so with Martinez in the outfield.

YEAR	TEAM	LVL	AGE	PA	DRC+	VORP	BABIP	BRR	FRAA	WARP
2018	DRG	RK	22	33	160	11.5	.571	2.2	CF(5): 0.4, LF(1): -0.2	0.5
2018	SPO	A-	22	273	103	16.4	.323	0.5	CF(55): 1.5, LF(2): 0.1	0.2
2019	TEX	MLB	23	251	16	-15.8	.151	0.2	CF 1, LF 0	-1.6

Leody Taveras CF
Born: 09/08/98   Age: 20   Bats: B   Throws: R
Height: 6'1"   Weight: 190   Origin: International Free Agent, 2015

YEAR	TEAM	LVL	AGE	PA	R	2B	3B	HR	RBI	BB	K	SB	CS	AVG/OBP/SLG
2016	DRN	RK	17	45	6	2	2	0	9	6	5	4	3	.385/.467/.538
2016	RNG	RK	17	155	22	6	3	1	15	11	24	11	4	.278/.329/.382
2016	SPO	A-	17	133	14	6	1	0	9	8	26	3	1	.228/.271/.293
2017	HIC	A	18	577	73	20	7	8	50	47	92	20	6	.249/.312/.360
2018	DEB	A+	19	580	65	16	7	5	48	51	96	19	11	.246/.312/.332
2019	TEX	MLB	20	251	23	4	1	5	18	9	59	3	1	.170/.199/.260

Breakout: 4%   Improve: 4%   Collapse: 0%   Attrition: 2%   MLB: 4%
Comparables: Cedric Hunter, Carlos Tocci, Billy McKinney

Taveras slugged .332 in High-A in 2018. That's not the season you want from a guy some considered to be the no. 1 prospect in the system coming into the year. Furthermore, that followed a 2017 in Low-A that wasn't exactly overwhelming. He's still just 20, so it's not time to panic yet, but his ability to adapt/grow/improve (likely in a repeat year at Down East) is going to be something to keep an eye on this year.

YEAR	TEAM	LVL	AGE	PA	DRC+	VORP	BABIP	BRR	FRAA	WARP
2016	DRN	RK	17	45	199	6.5	.441	-2.1	CF(7): -0.9, RF(2): -0.4	0.0
2016	RNG	RK	17	155	117	3.1	.328	-0.3	CF(31): -2.6, RF(3): -0.1	-0.2
2016	SPO	A-	17	133	72	2.4	.283	-0.3	CF(26): 2.1, LF(1): 0.0	-0.3
2017	HIC	A	18	577	98	17.7	.287	3.3	CF(125): -3.7, LF(3): -0.1	0.7
2018	DEB	A+	19	580	91	4.2	.292	0.3	CF(123): 7.0, RF(3): 0.0	0.8
2019	TEX	MLB	20	251	18	-14.8	.199	0.4	CF -1, LF 0	-1.7

Bubba Thompson CF

Born: 06/09/98 Age: 21 Bats: R Throws: R
Height: 6'2" Weight: 186 Origin: Round 1, 2017 Draft (#26 overall)

YEAR	TEAM	LVL	AGE	PA	R	2B	3B	HR	RBI	BB	K	SB	CS	AVG/OBP/SLG
2017	RNG	RK	19	123	23	7	2	3	12	6	28	5	5	.257/.317/.434
2018	HIC	A	20	363	52	18	5	8	42	23	104	32	7	.289/.344/.446
2019	TEX	MLB	21	251	27	7	1	6	19	3	90	7	2	.162/.174/.276

Breakout: 0% Improve: 3% Collapse: 0% Attrition: 2% MLB: 3%
Comparables: Teoscar Hernandez, Joe Benson, Michael Saunders

Thompson's stock after the 2018 season depends on whom you ask. Some in the Rangers organization suggest Thompson has surpassed Leody Taveras as their best position-player prospect, if not no. 1 overall. That's something of a surprise for a two-star athlete with just two years of professional ball under his belt, but the first-rounder's continued dominance in the Arizona Fall League did nothing to prove his believers wrong. He's likely to start 2019 in High-A Down East, but where he finishes the year is anyone's guess. (Unless your guess is "Saturn." Why would you guess that? It's not one of the options. Humans have never been to Saturn. You don't get to make any more guesses. Put down the book and go for a walk.)

YEAR	TEAM	LVL	AGE	PA	DRC+	VORP	BABIP	BRR	FRAA	WARP
2017	RNG	RK	19	123	80	3.9	.317	0.8	CF(27): -4.0	-0.6
2018	HIC	A	20	363	117	26.0	.396	6.1	CF(67): 1.1, LF(17): 0.7	1.9
2019	TEX	MLB	21	251	13	-15.7	.222	1.4	CF -1, LF 1	-1.7

Jose Trevino   C

Born: 11/28/92   Age: 26   Bats: R   Throws: R
Height: 5'11"   Weight: 211   Origin: Round 6, 2014 Draft (#186 overall)

YEAR	TEAM	LVL	AGE	PA	R	2B	3B	HR	RBI	BB	K	SB	CS	AVG/OBP/SLG
2016	HDS	A+	23	465	67	30	0	9	68	26	49	2	1	.303/.342/.434
2017	FRI	AA	24	423	39	12	0	7	42	19	44	1	2	.241/.275/.323
2018	TEX	MLB	25	8	0	0	0	0	3	0	1	0	0	.250/.250/.250
2018	FRI	AA	25	201	18	7	1	3	16	13	27	0	1	.234/.284/.332
2019	TEX	MLB	26	35	3	1	0	1	4	1	6	0	0	.206/.229/.324

Breakout: 9%   Improve: 21%   Collapse: 1%   Attrition: 14%   MLB: 25%
Comparables: Rob Johnson, Kyle Farmer, Jeff Frazier

Trevino made his big-league debut in 2018 and hit a walk-off single on Father's Day — his first since becoming a father himself, and five years after his own father's passing — for one of the most memorable moments in a forgettable Rangers season. He was back in the minors the next day, and suffered a (non-throwing) shoulder impingement that cost him the last two-plus months of the season. Trevino's defense has always been the catcher's calling card (he was the two-time minor-league Gold Glove winner), so the hope is that the injury won't affect his defense upon return — his bat isn't the type that would play at any other position. The Rangers still believe in Trevino, and if he sticks in the majors alongside Jeff Mathis, he'll benefit from a season under the tutelage of another defense-first, bat-occasionally catcher.

YEAR	TEAM	P. COUNT	FRM RUNS	BLK RUNS	THRW RUNS	TOT RUNS
2017	FRI	13448	24.9	4.7	0.5	30.2
2018	FRI	5456	6.0	0.5	0.6	6.7
2018	TEX	277	-0.2	-0.2	0.0	-0.6
2019	TEX	1284	1.0	0.2	0.0	1.2

YEAR	TEAM	LVL	AGE	PA	DRC+	VORP	BABIP	BRR	FRAA	WARP
2016	HDS	A+	23	465	115	26.3	.322	-1.3	C(100): 9.0	2.5
2017	FRI	AA	24	423	71	-0.7	.256	-0.1	C(99): 32.1	3.1
2018	TEX	MLB	25	8	82	-0.6	.286	0.0	C(3): -0.5	0.0
2018	FRI	AA	25	201	76	-0.7	.255	-0.8	C(38): 8.0	0.6
2019	TEX	MLB	26	35	45	-0.8	.242	-0.1	C 1	0.0

Jairo Beras RHP

Born: 12/25/94 Age: 24 Bats: R Throws: R
Height: 6'6" Weight: 195 Origin: International Free Agent, 2012

YEAR	TEAM	LVL	AGE	W	L	SV	G	GS	IP	H	HR	BB/9	K/9	K	GB%	BABIP
2017	HIC	A	22	0	1	0	13	0	13^1	11	2	6.1	9.4	14	26%	.250
2018	DEB	A+	23	3	2	3	38	0	54	35	4	4.3	12.5	75	35%	.261
2019	TEX	MLB	24	2	1	1	35	0	37^1	35	6	5.9	9.9	41	32%	.300

Breakout: 0% Improve: 1% Collapse: 2% Attrition: 2% MLB: 3%
Comparables: B.J. Rosenberg, A.J. Ramos, Anthony Slama

In the episode of *BoJack Horseman* in which BoJack is giving the eulogy at his mother's funeral, he talks about how he was sad when the show *Becker* got cancelled, not because it was a great show (it wasn't), but because it had all the *elements* of being a great show, but it never quite clicked. It wasn't that BoJack was mourning the loss of a show; he was mourning the loss of the hope that it would someday be great. Beras got a $4.5 million signing bonus in 2012 as an outfielder, and now he's a 24-year-old pitcher who hasn't played above High-A. The upside? He struck out 12.5 batters per nine innings for Down East last year.

YEAR	TEAM	LVL	AGE	WHIP	ERA	DRA	WARP	MPH	FB%	WHF	CSP
2017	HIC	A	22	1.50	5.40	3.47	0.2				
2018	DEB	A+	23	1.13	4.33	2.84	1.3				
2019	TEX	MLB	24	1.60	5.56	5.57	-0.3				

Hans Crouse RHP

Born: 09/15/98 Age: 20 Bats: L Throws: R
Height: 6'4" Weight: 180 Origin: Round 2, 2017 Draft (#66 overall)

YEAR	TEAM	LVL	AGE	W	L	SV	G	GS	IP	H	HR	BB/9	K/9	K	GB%	BABIP
2017	RNG	RK	18	0	0	0	10	6	20	7	1	3.2	13.5	30	60%	.176
2018	SPO	A-	19	5	1	0	8	8	38	25	2	2.6	11.1	47	36%	.253
2018	HIC	A	19	0	2	0	5	5	16.2	18	1	4.3	8.1	15	40%	.333
2019	TEX	MLB	20	2	3	0	12	9	37	40	8	5.1	8.8	36	40%	.307

Comparables: Carlos Carrasco, Eric Hurley, Anthony Swarzak

Hans Crouse is a tornado made up of smaller tornadoes. Just tornadoes all the way down. The tornadoes are on fire, and the fuel is distilled from the splinters of a thousand bats, rage-soaked in hate fluid and made brittle from the withering of 100 years under a vengeful sun, and the sun is Crouse, and you are his scorn made ash.

[Slackbot: #HFC]

Hans Crouse is a lava spawn, belched forth with the hatred of an earth that has grown to despise the little walking, crawling, singing things it used to love, and has now sworn an oath to consume them with its gargling maledictions.

[Slackbot: #HFC]

Hans Crouse is a visceral howl, a piercing prayer from a predator to the God who gave him the electric bristle of his hair, the tingling in his legs, the grind of his jaws, the blood of his prey and the sting of the brisk night air in his lungs, air made of gases that curl themselves into a supernova, exploding toward their ancestors.

[Slackbot: #HFC]

YEAR	TEAM	LVL	AGE	WHIP	ERA	DRA	WARP	MPH	FB%	WHF	CSP
2017	RNG	RK	18	0.70	0.45	2.04	0.8				
2018	SPO	A-	19	0.95	2.37	3.91	0.6				
2018	HIC	A	19	1.56	2.70	6.50	-0.3				
2019	TEX	MLB	20	1.64	6.11	6.14	-0.3				

Taylor Hearn LHP

Born: 08/30/94 Age: 24 Bats: L Throws: L
Height: 6'5" Weight: 210 Origin: Round 5, 2015 Draft (#164 overall)

YEAR	TEAM	LVL	AGE	W	L	SV	G	GS	IP	H	HR	BB/9	K/9	K	GB%	BABIP
2016	NAT	RK	21	0	0	0	2	2	6.1	2	1	8.5	11.4	8	55%	.100
2016	HAG	A	21	1	0	0	8	2	22.2	25	3	2.8	12.3	31	39%	.393
2016	WVA	A	21	1	1	0	8	3	22.2	15	2	4.0	14.3	36	47%	.289
2017	BRD	A+	22	4	6	0	18	17	87.1	65	8	3.8	10.9	106	50%	.281
2018	ALT	AA	23	3	6	0	19	19	104	75	6	3.3	9.3	107	41%	.256
2018	FRI	AA	23	1	2	0	5	5	25	29	5	3.2	11.9	33	36%	.375
2019	TEX	MLB	24	2	2	0	6	6	30	29	5	4.4	9.3	31	40%	.295

Breakout: 13% Improve: 26% Collapse: 15% Attrition: 36% MLB: 50%
Comparables: P.J. Walters, Hunter Wood, Jake Arrieta

Hearn, a native Texan, was part of the Rangers' return for Keone Kela at the 2018 deadline. Texas gave up their 25-year-old closer for a nearly-24-year-old left-handed starter. Hearn is the grandson of famous rodeo cowboy Cleo Hearn, who was also the first African-American Marlboro Man, and Taylor participated in youth rodeos, competing in calf-roping until he was in his late teens, when he quit to focus on baseball. So yeah, Arlington seems like a good fit. Oh right, also the fact that the Rangers desperately needed young starting pitchers with legitimate rotation upside.

YEAR	TEAM	LVL	AGE	WHIP	ERA	DRA	WARP	MPH	FB%	WHF	CSP
2016	NAT	RK	21	1.26	1.42	1.51	0.3				
2016	HAG	A	21	1.41	3.18	2.22	0.7				
2016	WVA	A	21	1.10	1.99	1.97	0.8				
2017	BRD	A+	22	1.17	4.12	3.37	1.9				
2018	ALT	AA	23	1.09	3.12	3.61	2.1				
2018	FRI	AA	23	1.52	5.04	4.29	0.3				
2019	TEX	MLB	24	1.47	5.00	5.12	0.1				

Jonathan Hernandez   RHP

Born: 07/06/96   Age: 22   Bats: R   Throws: R
Height: 6'2"   Weight: 175   Origin: International Free Agent, 2013

YEAR	TEAM	LVL	AGE	W	L	SV	G	GS	IP	H	HR	BB/9	K/9	K	GB%	BABIP
2016	HIC	A	19	10	9	0	24	22	116^1	110	14	3.8	6.6	85	49%	.279
2017	HIC	A	20	2	5	0	9	9	46^1	55	5	2.5	8.9	46	48%	.370
2017	DEB	A+	20	3	6	0	14	13	65^1	66	2	4.3	8.8	64	47%	.350
2018	DEB	A+	21	4	2	0	10	10	57^1	37	6	2.7	12.1	77	52%	.263
2018	FRI	AA	21	4	4	0	12	12	64	58	6	5.1	8.0	57	51%	.299
2019	TEX	MLB	22	5	7	0	19	19	96^2	92	12	4.6	8.9	95	44%	.305

Breakout: 14%   Improve: 21%   Collapse: 6%   Attrition: 24%   MLB: 34%
Comparables: Jordan Walden, Sean Reid-Foley, Jake Thompson

Hernandez spent the first half of 2018 on a personal mission to embarrass High-A hitters as a member of the Down East Wood Ducks, then started the second half with an extended lesson on the difference between High-A and Double-A. He turned a corner in August, however: In his last four starts, he racked up an 0.97 WHIP and a 1.14 ERA, striking out 27 and walking 10 over 23 2/3 innings. More importantly, he showed improvement on all four of his pitches, giving hope that he will be a starter and not just a relief option.

YEAR	TEAM	LVL	AGE	WHIP	ERA	DRA	WARP	MPH	FB%	WHF	CSP
2016	HIC	A	19	1.37	4.56	3.64	1.9				
2017	HIC	A	20	1.47	4.86	3.21	1.1				
2017	DEB	A+	20	1.48	3.44	4.00	1.0				
2018	DEB	A+	21	0.94	2.20	2.39	2.0				
2018	FRI	AA	21	1.47	4.92	4.46	0.7				
2019	TEX	MLB	22	1.47	4.71	4.67	0.9				

Wei-Chieh Huang RHP

Born: 09/26/93 Age: 25 Bats: R Throws: R
Height: 6'1" Weight: 170 Origin: International Free Agent, 2014

YEAR	TEAM	LVL	AGE	W	L	SV	G	GS	IP	H	HR	BB/9	K/9	K	GB%	BABIP
2016	VIS	A+	22	1	1	0	6	6	26^1	33	5	4.1	8.5	25	44%	.346
2016	YAK	A-	22	2	2	0	9	4	30^1	33	4	3.3	12.5	42	39%	.382
2017	KNC	A	23	1	1	0	20	0	40	25	2	2.2	10.6	47	39%	.235
2017	VIS	A+	23	1	0	1	10	0	24^2	15	0	3.6	11.7	32	38%	.259
2018	VIS	A+	24	4	1	0	19	0	31^1	17	3	4.6	13.2	46	41%	.230
2018	WTN	AA	24	2	1	1	10	2	27	20	1	2.3	10.7	32	42%	.297
2018	FRI	AA	24	1	1	0	9	0	20	21	5	3.6	11.2	25	36%	.320
2019	TEX	MLB	25	1	1	0	16	0	17	15	2	4.4	9.9	19	37%	.292

Breakout: 10%   Improve: 14%   Collapse: 16%   Attrition: 26%   MLB: 34%
Comparables: Daniel Slania, Buddy Baumann, Tayron Guerrero

As baseball continues to remold and reshape the definitions of words like *starter*, *opener*, *primary pitcher* and *rotation*, it will be interesting to see the value of guys like Huang, whose role in Arizona (before being traded to Texas in the Jake Diekman deal) was to pitch two to four innings every two to four days. It's like a swingman, but intentionally not relying on a starter to crash and burn first. Texas was intrigued enough by the concept to keep him on basically the same schedule once he arrived, and while the results in Frisco weren't overwhelming, or even particularly good, the Rangers liked him enough to put him on the 40-man roster in advance of the Rule 5 draft.

YEAR	TEAM	LVL	AGE	WHIP	ERA	DRA	WARP	MPH	FB%	WHF	CSP
2016	VIS	A+	22	1.71	6.49	4.92	0.2				
2016	YAK	A-	22	1.45	5.34	2.75	0.8				
2017	KNC	A	23	0.88	1.58	2.62	1.1				
2017	VIS	A+	23	1.01	2.19	2.80	0.6				
2018	VIS	A+	24	1.05	2.59	2.67	0.8				
2018	WTN	AA	24	1.00	2.00	2.67	0.7				
2018	FRI	AA	24	1.45	6.30	2.62	0.6				
2019	TEX	MLB	25	1.37	4.56	4.55	0.1				

Mike Matuella RHP
Born: 06/03/94 Age: 25 Bats: R Throws: R
Height: 6'6" Weight: 220 Origin: Round 3, 2015 Draft (#78 overall)

YEAR	TEAM	LVL	AGE	W	L	SV	G	GS	IP	H	HR	BB/9	K/9	K	GB%	BABIP
2017	HIC	A	23	4	6	0	21	20	75	88	6	2.8	7.2	60	50%	.350
2018	DEB	A+	24	3	5	2	20	8	51^1	67	12	3.7	7.7	44	51%	.327
2019	TEX	MLB	25	2	4	0	17	10	48^2	58	8	4.8	6.0	32	45%	.314

Breakout: 3% Improve: 5% Collapse: 1% Attrition: 4% MLB: 7%
Comparables: Daniel Davidson, Brandon Mann, Eddie Bonine

The Rangers hoped for a breakout season from Matuella at High-A. Instead, he got knocked around so badly that the team moved him to the bullpen after eight starts, then shut him down completely in July. He's not old enough to panic just yet, but if you haven't slammed the brakes on your Matuella Hype Train, you might have noticed it feels like you're floating around the car? That's because you blew through an unfinished bridge. The rest of us will be holding tight here and letting the kids run around in the grass while Matuella does his best to get the bridge finished in 2019 so we can get this thing back on the move.

YEAR	TEAM	LVL	AGE	WHIP	ERA	DRA	WARP	MPH	FB%	WHF	CSP
2017	HIC	A	23	1.48	4.20	6.33	-0.9				
2018	DEB	A+	24	1.71	8.24	5.88	-0.4				
2019	TEX	MLB	25	1.73	6.06	6.08	-0.4				

Joe Palumbo LHP

Born: 10/26/94 Age: 24 Bats: L Throws: L
Height: 6'1" Weight: 168 Origin: Round 30, 2013 Draft (#910 overall)

YEAR	TEAM	LVL	AGE	W	L	SV	G	GS	IP	H	HR	BB/9	K/9	K	GB%	BABIP
2016	HIC	A	21	7	5	8	33	7	96^1	71	5	3.4	11.4	122	52%	.287
2017	DEB	A+	22	1	0	0	3	3	13^2	4	0	2.6	14.5	22	58%	.167
2018	DEB	A+	23	1	4	0	6	6	27	24	3	2.0	11.3	34	42%	.304
2018	FRI	AA	23	1	0	0	2	2	9^1	6	0	2.9	9.6	10	39%	.261
2019	TEX	MLB	24	2	3	0	17	6	41	38	5	3.9	9.5	44	44%	.297

Breakout: 15% Improve: 22% Collapse: 3% Attrition: 18% MLB: 30%
Comparables: Glenn Sparkman, Taylor Williams, Glen Perkins

The Rangers' next wave of young starting pitching is a few years away: Hans Crouse, Cole Ragans, Kyle Cody and others aren't likely to see time in Globe Life Park before the team heads across the street to the shiny new stadium. Palumbo may be the exception. There were whispers that he might make the jump from High-A to the big leagues in 2017 before Tommy John surgery put him in timeout for a year. Texas took it nice and easy with Palumbo in 2018, letting him work his way up to Double-A for his last two starts. While 6-foot-1 and 168 pounds isn't the typical build you expect from a top starting-pitching prospect, so far ... [points back in time to C.J. Wilson, then back to Palumbo] ... he seems fine.

YEAR	TEAM	LVL	AGE	WHIP	ERA	DRA	WARP	MPH	FB%	WHF	CSP
2016	HIC	A	21	1.11	2.24	2.49	2.7				
2017	DEB	A+	22	0.59	0.66	2.80	0.4				
2018	DEB	A+	23	1.11	2.67	3.01	0.7				
2018	FRI	AA	23	0.96	1.93	3.72	0.2				
2019	TEX	MLB	24	1.38	4.31	4.39	0.5				

Tyler Phillips RHP
Born: 10/27/97   Age: 21   Bats: R   Throws: R
Height: 6'5"   Weight: 200   Origin: Round 16, 2015 Draft (#468 overall)

YEAR	TEAM	LVL	AGE	W	L	SV	G	GS	IP	H	HR	BB/9	K/9	K	GB%	BABIP
2016	SPO	A-	18	4	7	0	13	13	58²	78	2	3.1	8.7	57	53%	.388
2017	HIC	A	19	1	2	0	7	4	25¹	28	2	3.2	5.3	15	47%	.302
2017	SPO	A-	19	4	2	0	13	13	73	78	6	1.4	9.6	78	52%	.338
2018	HIC	A	20	11	5	0	22	22	128	117	4	1.0	8.7	124	54%	.308
2019	TEX	MLB	21	5	7	0	19	19	99²	111	16	3.2	7.0	78	44%	.308

Breakout: 7%   Improve: 12%   Collapse: 5%   Attrition: 11%   MLB: 18%
Comparables: Nick Kingham, Michael Bowden, Jameson Taillon

Here's what you need to know about Phillips: He struck out 124 hitters in 128 innings at Hickory last year, and walked just 14. Given how his first turn in Hickory went in 2017 — when he gave up, like, a million runs — that's quite an improvement. As for the why? First, his demeanor calmed down quite a bit. Second, his changeup started humming, making a mockery of hitters every time it got in the vicinity of the plate. So badly did it embarrass batters that it started to make onlookers uncomfortable at the mean-spirited nature of it all. They started feeling bad and yelling things like, "It's okay, we can tell you're trying very hard!" and, "I'm sure you're quite good at other things!" But the hitters thought it was sarcasm and it made the whole thing worse.

YEAR	TEAM	LVL	AGE	WHIP	ERA	DRA	WARP	MPH	FB%	WHF	CSP
2016	SPO	A-	18	1.67	6.44	3.57	1.2				
2017	HIC	A	19	1.46	6.39	5.88	-0.2				
2017	SPO	A-	19	1.22	3.45	3.28	1.7				
2018	HIC	A	20	1.02	2.67	3.10	3.2				
2019	TEX	MLB	21	1.46	5.17	5.15	0.4				

Drew Smyly LHP
Born: 06/13/89 Age: 30 Bats: L Throws: L
Height: 6'3" Weight: 190 Origin: Round 2, 2010 Draft (#68 overall)

YEAR	TEAM	LVL	AGE	W	L	SV	G	GS	IP	H	HR	BB/9	K/9	K	GB%	BABIP
2016	TBA	MLB	27	7	12	0	30	30	175[1]	174	32	2.5	8.6	167	33%	.291
2019	TEX	MLB	30	7	9	0	23	23	131	132	26	3.6	8.9	130	36%	.294

Breakout: 22% Improve: 47% Collapse: 11% Attrition: 12% MLB: 85%
Comparables: John Patterson, Scott Baker, Brandon Morrow

If Scott Boras was putting together a promotional binder for Smyly, he would undoubtedly point out that the left-hander struck out every single batter he faced in 2018. The observer with less of an agenda might note that those batters were all members of the Bowling Green Hot Rods in the Midwest League, and that there were just three of them. The Cubs would not have expected much from Smyly in the first season of the two-year deal they signed him to, but they likely expected something, given that his Tommy John surgery took place in June 2017 and he was facing hitters just over a year later. Setbacks and caution on the part of the team limited him to that single professional inning, so Smyly will have to prove his health in 2019. Hopefully a binder with quite such a high degree of creativity won't be required next offseason.

YEAR	TEAM	LVL	AGE	WHIP	ERA	DRA	WARP	MPH	FB%	WHF	CSP
2016	TBA	MLB	27	1.27	4.88	4.66	1.4	92.7	56.9	11.9	45.4
2019	TEX	MLB	30	1.41	5.14	5.27	0.2	92.0	56.7	11.8	45.3

LINEOUTS

Hitters

HITTER	POS	TEAM	LVL	AGE	PA	R	2B	3B	HR	RBI	BB	K	SB	CS	AVG/OBP/SLG	DRC+	WARP
Michael Chirinos	3B	DRG	Rk	18	298	47	7	3	2	42	49	20	13	4	.318/.431/.397	166	2.6
Chase d'Arnaud	INF	SAC	AAA	31	300	54	14	4	12	43	40	65	15	3	.292/.393/.522	136	1.5
	INF	SFN	MLB	31	100	9	5	0	3	9	4	37	2	1	.215/.253/.366	71	-0.2
Zack Granite	OF	ROC	AAA	25	263	28	8	0	0	4	22	28	9	4	.211/.282/.245	68	0.3
Sam Huff	C	HIC	A	20	448	53	22	3	18	55	23	140	9	1	.241/.292/.439	97	0.4
Eric Jenkins	LF	HIC	A	21	113	14	1	3	3	15	8	32	16	3	.291/.339/.447	114	0.3
	LF	DEB	A+	21	301	36	6	4	1	14	21	79	19	5	.223/.282/.285	66	-0.9
Adam Moore	C	DUR	AAA	34	208	18	11	1	4	30	11	50	0	0	.219/.260/.347	65	-0.7
	C	TBA	MLB	34	20	2	1	0	1	2	1	7	0	0	.222/.263/.444	77	-0.2
Jonathan Ornelas	3B	RNG	Rk	18	203	34	10	4	3	28	25	41	15	5	.302/.389/.459	139	0.9
Anderson Tejeda	SS	DEB	A+	20	522	76	17	5	19	74	49	142	11	4	.259/.331/.439	120	2.9
Eli White	INF	MID	AA	24	578	81	30	8	9	55	62	116	18	9	.306/.388/.450	132	3.3

Texas claimed **Carlos Asuaje** off waivers from San Diego in December, but the glove-first utility infielder had already agreed to sign with a team in Korea. ⓧ **Michael Chirinos** walked 49 times in 298 plate appearances as an 18-year-old in the Dominican Summer League. With just two homers, pitchers weren't working around him. Dude just has a good eye. ⓧ There's a little Justin Turner in **Chase d'Arnaud**'s new lift-oriented swing, but it was undone by all the Chase d'Arnaud in his old whiff-prone approach. ⓧ **Anthony Gose** throws 99 mph from the left side, and while a few teams wanted him to stick to doing that, the Rangers allowed him to also play outfield and hit. His numbers weren't particularly encouraging on either front. ⓧ **Zack Granite** hit rock bottom in 2018, in large part thanks to a shoulder injury, but still has plenty of speed and draws enough walks for a backup outfielder. ⓧ It's not impossible to make it to the big leagues as a 6-foot-4 catcher (Joe Mauer, stand up, but watch your head) but **Sam Huff**'s odds of staying there would be better if he shrank a few inches. The good news: He may have the pop to withstand a move to first base. ⓧ **Eric Jenkins** destroyed Single-A pitching when he first arrived, but that was way back in 2015. It took him two more full seasons at the level before he finally got out of neutral in 2018 and earned a call-up to Down East. ⓧ **Adam Moore** is not allowed in Canada and may not be allowed in the major leagues again either. ⓧ The Other **Rougned Odor** has still yet to play stateside. Also, whatever happened to Ozzie Canseco? (Ozzie Canseco earned his 50th five-star ride as an Uber driver in July 2018. This is real; you can find it on Twitter.) ⓧ **Jonathan Ornelas** was the 91st pick in the 2018 draft, and he has very quickly caught the attention of anyone who has seen him play. Drafted as a shortstop, he'll likely be a third baseman, meaning he'll need to hit. Fortunately, he can *hit*. ⓧ The longest pop song ever recorded is 69 minutes and contains over 500 verses. It's called "The Devil Glitch" and we'll assume every verse goes something like: "He's like *this* close / so have no fear / this'll be **Ryan Rua**'s breakout year." ⓧ **Anderson Tejeda**, playing at High-A for the first time, not only improved his defense, but increased his pop at the plate, hitting a career-high 19 home runs. Unfortunately, he also struck out 142 times. ⓧ **Eli White** has just enough power, speed, defensive chops and versatility to back up six positions. Don't knock it 'til you've tried *not* having guys like this in your system.

Pitchers

PITCHER	TEAM	LVL	AGE	W	L	SV	G	GS	IP	H	HR	BB/9	K/9	K	GB%	WHIP	ERA	DRA	WARP
A.J. Alexy	HIC	A	20	6	8	0	22	20	108	89	5	4.3	11.5	138	35%	1.31	3.58	4.12	1.4
Kyle Bird	MNT	AA	25	0	2	4	16	1	19²	14	2	4.1	10.5	23	43%	1.17	3.66	2.45	0.6
	DUR	AAA	25	3	1	0	27	5	55²	38	4	4.2	10.5	65	40%	1.15	1.94	3.43	1.1
Brock Burke	PCH	A+	21	3	5	0	16	13	82	85	4	3.3	9.5	87	48%	1.40	3.84	4.03	1.2
	MNT	AA	21	6	1	0	9	9	55¹	39	2	2.3	11.5	71	37%	0.96	1.95	3.22	1.4
Zac Curtis	PHI	MLB	25	0	0	0	7	0	9²	6	0	9.3	9.3	10	44%	1.66	1.86	7.75	-0.3
	LEH	AAA	25	3	2	0	33	0	42	29	4	4.7	10.3	48	44%	1.21	3.00	3.25	0.9
	ROU	AAA	25	1	0	0	9	0	9	5	1	6.0	12.0	12	47%	1.22	4.00	3.22	0.2
	TEX	MLB	25	0	1	0	8	0	6²	6	1	12.1	10.8	8	22%	2.25	9.45	7.78	-0.2
Miguel Del Pozo	JAX	AA	25	5	0	1	28	0	34	37	3	4.0	9.0	34	39%	1.53	3.97	4.50	0.2
Luke Farrell	CHN	MLB	27	3	4	0	20	2	31¹	30	7	4.6	11.2	39	31%	1.47	5.17	4.27	0.3
	IOW	AAA	27	1	4	0	12	12	54¹	40	4	4.6	10.1	61	40%	1.25	3.64	3.58	1.2
Nick Gardewine	TEX	MLB	24	0	0	0	3	0	5	7	0	0.0	7.2	4	22%	1.40	3.60	7.41	-0.1
	ROU	AAA	24	2	1	1	12	0	12¹	15	1	5.1	12.4	17	42%	1.78	7.30	3.30	0.3
Jeanmar Gomez	CHR	AAA	30	5	0	2	30	0	40	35	2	2.9	7.9	35	56%	1.20	2.03	3.85	0.6
	CHA	MLB	30	0	2	0	26	0	25	29	3	3.6	9.7	27	40%	1.56	4.68	3.22	0.5
Brett Martin	FRI	AA	23	2	10	0	29	15	89	138	7	2.9	9.7	96	50%	1.88	7.28	4.68	0.6
Zach McAllister	CLE	MLB	30	1	2	0	41	0	41²	47	7	2.2	7.3	34	43%	1.37	4.97	4.44	0.2
	DET	MLB	30	0	0	0	3	0	3¹	10	1	0.0	13.5	5	36%	3.00	21.60	4.81	0.0
	OKL	AAA	30	1	1	0	5	0	6	6	0	3.0	13.5	9	40%	1.33	9.00	3.46	0.1
Sergio Pacheco	DRG	Rk	18	4	2	1	13	11	65¹	54	0	1.2	8.1	59	58%	0.96	2.07	3.50	1.8
Connor Sadzeck	ROU	AAA	26	5	3	0	32	0	38	36	2	3.8	10.2	43	45%	1.37	4.03	3.41	0.7
	TEX	MLB	26	0	0	0	13	2	9¹	6	0	10.6	6.8	7	42%	1.82	0.96	7.56	-0.3
Alex Speas	HIC	A	20	2	0	6	20	0	28²	16	1	6.6	15.4	49	56%	1.29	2.20	1.43	1.2

One of the "other" returns for Yu Darvish, **A.J. Alexy** spent 2018 repeating Single-A, and wasn't markedly better than he had been in 2017. That's not to say he's a bust; any time a starter has 11.5 K/9 rate at any level, he's still a dude, and Alexy threw more strikes for the Crawdads than he did the previous season. ⚾ Along with Isiah Kiner-Falefa, **Austin Bibens-Dirkx** became part of the first all-hyphen battery in big-league history. ⚾ Grandson of Big, nephew of Larry, little brother of Sue and Greg, **Kyle Bird** is going to open a game in 2019. ⚾ In a feel-good story, **Clayton Blackburn** started the Rangers' first spring-training game, a tip of the cap by manager Jeff Banister to the native Texan who grew up a Rangers fan. Alas, Blackburn suffered a season-ending elbow injury before March was even halfway done and Banister was unemployed by Thanksgiving. ⚾ **Brock Burke** was the Rays' minor-league pitcher of the year in 2018 and has added velocity since being drafted in 2014. ⚾ After coming over to Texas as the lone big leaguer in the Cole Hamels trade, **Eddie Butler** proceeded to get knocked around, eat a bunch of relief innings and get dropped from the 40-man roster, later undergoing surgery for a "core injury." ⚾ **Kyle Cody** was the Rangers' 2017 minor league pitcher of the year, and was poised to take a huge step forward in 2018. Instead, elbow discomfort kept him off the mound for months and foretold a mid-July Tommy John surgery. ⚾ The only thing wilder than **Zac Curtis**' hair is his fastball ... is what a mean person would say. The lefty has undeniable swing-and-miss stuff, but the walks proved too much for the Texas front office to keep him on the 40-man; he was still a free agent at press time. ⚾ Hitting the mid-90s from the left side, **Miguel Del Pozo** uses good extension to get on top of hitters. Paired with his breaking stuff, he averages a strikeout an inning with average control. ⚾ Further proof that all of us are a little imperfect, **Luke Farrell** has trouble getting his pitches in the desired spots. But when he does, the batter also misses the mark. The inconsistency both ways is why Farrell has become a prolific waiver selection. ⚾ The Rangers gambled on Mike Minor, Matt Moore and **Doug Fister** in their 2018 rotation, and hit on one of them. "One" is also the number of wins Fister earned before missing the last four months with a hip injury. ⚾ Injuries limited **Nick Gardewine** to just over 17 innings, karmic retribution for his spring-training admission that he'd never heard of Hank Williams Sr. ⚾ Finding out that journeyman reliever **Jeanmar Gomez**—an avowed sinkerballer in the age of the letter-high four-seam fastball—posted the highest strikeout rate of his career in an otherwise unremarkable, up-and-down campaign for a 100-loss White Sox team: That's the kind of fun factoid you get in return for purchasing this book, provided you turned to this exact page. ⚾ **Ronald Herrera** has been traded for Kyle Blanks, Jose Pirela and Reiver Sanmartin, and will somehow turn just 24 in May. We need fun facts because he didn't make it off the disabled list in 2018. ⚾ **Kevin Jepsen** was a great comeback story in spring training. Kevin Jepsen was not a great comeback story in the regular season. ⚾ **Brandon Mann** made his big-league debut just a few days before turning 34, after 16 years in the minor leagues, independent leagues, Japanese leagues, Japanese independent leagues and one year when he shaved extra close and played high school ball as "Brayden Teenn." ⚾ **Brett Martin** looked great in spring training, then looked decidedly less great at Double-A Frisco, where he landed in the bullpen. ⚾ Not much went right in 2018 for **Zach McAllister**, but after two DFAs and three teams in the span of three weeks, at least he got to add a couple extra jerseys to his collection. ⚾ After a disappointing 2017, most Mets fans wanted **Rafael Montero**, the former top prospect turned maddeningly inconsistent fifth starter, off the roster. The Mets outrighted him in November, and he elected free agency, which led to a minor-league deal with Texas, where he'll finish his rehab in the hopes of a mid-2019 return. ⚾ **Sergio Pacheco** made it stateside for the first time when he was part of the Rangers' fall instructional league contingency. He walked just 21 batters across 147 Dominican Summer League innings (though he did plunk 14 more). ⚾ **Ricardo Rodriguez** was injured for the beginning (biceps tendinitis) and end (shoulder impingement) of 2018, and despite being effective in the minor leagues in the interim, he was non-tendered after the season. ⚾ While his walks were still a problem, big right-hander **Connor Sadzeck** showed a lot more poise in his time in Arlington than he had in Surprise. ⚾ This **Alex Speas** kid is putting up numbers like 2017 Joe Palumb ... oh. Tommy John surgery in June shelved the flamethrower for the remainder of 2018 and at least the first half of 2019. His walk rate was too high as a starter and hasn't been a lot lower as a reliever, but the strikeout and ground-ball rates were up. ⚾ **Chris Tillman** was technically a member of the Texas Rangers organization in 2018! He pitched at Triple-A Round Rock. This concludes the list of interesting Chris Tillman facts from this year's annual. ⚾ **Edinson Volquez** is back where he started, and it might just be the push he needs to get that Rookie of the Year award.

Rangers Prospects

The State of the System:
The Rangers system is back on the upswing, and you will be shocked to learn it is due to an abundance of toolsy up-the-middle bats and young, hard-throwing arms.

The Top Ten:

1 **Leody Taveras OF** OFP: 60   Likely: 50   ETA: 2021
Born: 09/08/98   Age: 20   Bats: B   Throws: R   Height: 6'1"   Weight: 190
Origin: International Free Agent, 2015

The Report: He's dead so we can't be sure Kant wasn't writing about Leody Taveras in his *Critique of Judgement* when he opined: "The judgement of taste is therefore not a judgement of cognition, and is consequently not logical but aesthetical, by which we can understand that whose determining ground can be *no other than subjective*."

When considering aesthetics, Kant further delves into the beautiful versus the pleasant versus the good.

The Pleasant: "As regards the Pleasant, therefore, the fundamental proposition is valid: *Every one has his own taste.*" The first time I saw Taveras I was running late to the park. Got out of the house tardy, hit traffic on the Garden State, barely got to my seat in Lakewood for the anthem, stuffing rosters into my backpack as I traipsed down the concourse. I don't like to be frazzled. I don't like to miss BP. I caught Taveras in the on-deck circle out of the corner of my eye, taking a couple practice cuts. "One man likes the tone of wind instruments, another that of strings." I like *this*.

The Beautiful: "In all judgements by which we describe anything as beautiful, we allow no one to be of another opinion." Now we touch on universality for a moment. We've never been particularly out of step with the industry on Taveras. The glove, arm, and run tools make him a good bet to at least have Leonys Martin's career. Nor were we the first to sing his praises in particularly hushed tones. Craig Goldstein—I don't know if you remember him—whispered to me about his spring training BPs in 2016.

The Good: "In respect to the Good it is true that judgments make rightful claim to validity for every one; but the Good is represented only *by means of a concept* as the object of a universal satisfaction." I don't remember if it was KG or Parks who said the only goal of a farm system is to convert it into major-league talent. I suppose Kant would call this "purposiveness."

I may lean more towards the transcendental philosopher than the logician end of the spectrum of prospect writing, but I can assure those looking for universality of satisfaction with any prospect, here you will only find pedantry. Oh, and a dude who never gives up on this tools profile.

The Risks: High. His best stateside performance was a .711 OPS in the launching pad of the AZL. All the drool-worthy batting practice swings in the world can't paper over the risk here.

Ben Carsley's Fantasy Take: We've been aggressive in our rankings of Taveras on the fantasy side as well (no. 34 on our midseason top-50), and the tools are still drool-worthy. That being said, I imagine Bret Sayre and I will be butting heads a bit on Taveras when it comes to our 2019 list. I still like Taveras quite a bit, but we're getting to the point where I'm going to value some guys who've actually performed in the high minors above Taveras, who is pretty much still just the idea of a good fantasy prospect at this point. I'm not being alarmist—Taveras is still an easy top-100 and maybe a top-50 guy for me—but he's not the top-25 dynasty prospect I'd hoped we'd all view him as by now.

2 Bubba Thompson OF

OFP: 60   Likely: 50   ETA: 2022
Born: 06/09/98   Age: 21   Bats: R   Throws: R   Height: 6'2"   Weight: 186
Origin: Round 1, 2017 Draft (#26 overall)

The Report: The Rangers have a history of drafting toolsy athletic outfielders from the South who have questionable hit tools, and at first glance Thompson looks the part. He has one of the best body projections in baseball, as he stands at 6-foot-2 with broad shoulders, an athletic build, and lean muscle throughout with room for growth. Thompson is an elite athlete with quick twitch and explosiveness in the hips and wrists. At any given moment he can burst into movement, whether it's into a sprint or firing his hips in a swing.

Unlike the Rangers draft picks of yore, Bubba has an instinctual feel for getting his bat on the ball and the ability to turn on velocity. Thompson generates plus bat speed with a swing plane that generally results in line drives on his hard contact, although he collapses his torso a bit to get a higher launch angle on pitches low and in. Thompson has plus raw power and could grow into more without losing athleticism or flexibility. With his swing, he probably won't tap into all of it, but he still should generate average power at the highest level.

The main concern with the offensive profile is his pitch recognition, as he struggles to pick up off-speed and spin. Thompson is a double-plus runner with a body that suggests he'll stay that way, and he's improving as a baserunner.

That speed and a plus arm allow Bubba to make up for his inconsistent reads and routes in the outfield, and with improvement he should be above-average in center or plus in a corner. Ultimately, Thompson profiles as an average center fielder with the upside for much more depending on how much he is able to polish his pitch recognition and zone control at the plate.

The Risks: High. He's young, far away, the power may or may not show up, and he ran a pretty high strikeout rate in A-ball.

Ben Carsley's Fantasy Take: Yes please. See that part about double-plus speed? That means we don't need Thompson to even hit the average power projection to be very invested in him as a dynasty league asset. I realize that the lead time is a little longer than we'd prefer, but Thompson's defense gives him a reasonably high chance of making the majors, and you've got to like the above report about his feel for hitting. One of the most common questions we get every offseason is "which low minor leaguer could make a big jump in value this season?" and Thompson definitely qualifies.

3

Julio Pablo Martinez   OF OFP: 60   Likely: 50
ETA: Your guess is as good as ours. 2020?
Born: 03/21/96   Age: 23   Bats: L   Throws: L   Height: 5'9"   Weight: 174
Origin: International Free Agent, 2018

The Report: When you miss out on signing Shohei Ohtani and have a couple million bucks to burn, there are worse places to impulse-buy than the toolsy Cuban outfielder aisle. Martinez fits right into the Rangers system with his plus athletic tools and plus bat speed. He gets more pop out of his smallish frame than you'd expect, but there's some length to get to it and he struggled a bit more than you'd hope for a 22-year-old in the Northwest League, stateside debut or not. But his speed and potential above-average glove in center field will grant him plenty of time to figure out pro pitching, not unlike the two names ahead of him.

The Risks: High. There's a huge delta here until we get a feel for how he will handle better pitching.

Ben Carsley's Fantasy Take: From a fantasy perspective, Martinez profiles pretty damn similarly to Taveras at this point. While the former may have better future projections on the hit tool, the latter has a slightly better ETA. Expect Martinez to rank in middle of the top-101 in some sort of tier of toolsy outfielders, and consider him one of the more attractive additions to the MiLB talent pool for those of you about to hold preseason drafts.

4

Anderson Tejeda   SS OFP: 60   Likely: 50
ETA: He's moving a level a year. 2020
Born: 05/01/98   Age: 21   Bats: L   Throws: R   Height: 5'11"   Weight: 185
Origin: International Free Agent, 2014

The Report: That went a bit better. We aggressively placed Tejeda on the 2017 101—perhaps too aggressively—based on strong looks out of the Northwest League. He then struggled in full-season ball, showing typical teenager warts like over-aggressiveness at the plate and mixed reliability in the field. But a strong showing in the High-A Carolina League last year saw Tejeda's stock rise to, and even surpass, where it was two winters ago.

Even now, Tejeda is a Very Rangers Prospect, and we mean that in ways both good and bad. You can probably envision him in your head if you've followed the Rangers system long enough. He's athletic and projectable, but also short. We slap the "good feel for hitting" euphemism on him a lot because we think he'll hit for average eventually, even though he hasn't done so yet. He has plus raw power that he actualized into games this year, as we'd suspected he would for a couple years, and he has really good bat speed. He'll show a strong enough first step and arm to give him a chance to not just stick at shortstop but be pretty good there.

He's also still too undisciplined at the plate, which leads to too much swing-and-miss. It's not as bad as it looked in 2017, and we're optimistic that he'll continue to improve here as he ages. But if it all falls apart for Tejeda offensively against upper-level pitching, well, don't say we didn't warn you.

The Risks: Moderate. As A-ballers go, we're pretty confident Tejeda is a major leaguer, given that the framework for a versatile power-hitting infield reserve is more or less already present. We also think he's got a shot to be a lot more. There's some fuzziness on exactly what type of player he'll be, which mostly depends on whether the hit tool spikes and which way the body goes.

Ben Carsley's Fantasy Take: Shortstop isn't quite the barren wasteland it was for fantasy owners a few years back, but it's still not a very deep position. Consider, for example, that Jose Peraza, Jonathan Villar and Adalberto Mondesi were all top-15 shortstops last year, per ESPN's Player Rater. The catch? All of those guys put up big stolen base numbers, and while Tejeda may run a bit he's not a burner. That means he's gonna have to take more of the 2019 Marcus Semien/Gleyber Torres/Jurickson Profar path to value, in which well-rounded contributions and non-embarrassing batting averages win the day. This is a long-winded way of saying Tejeda would have to really, really click to become a top-10 shortstop, but top-20 seems well within his grasp if he stays on his current trajectory.

5 Taylor Hearn LHP   OFP: 60   Likely: 50

ETA: Late 2019 as a reliever, 2020 as a starter
Born: 08/30/94   Age: 24   Bats: L   Throws: L   Height: 6'5"   Weight: 210
Origin: Round 5, 2015 Draft (#164 overall)

The Report: The first thing that stands out on Hearn's scouting report is, well, the ol' number one. It's a potentially plus-plus mid-90s howitzer with nasty cutting action. He'll bore it into righties with malice of forethought. Hearn will mix in a low-90s two-seamer for an armside look as well. He made strides with his breaking ball, a power 11-6 breaker in the low-80s. It will flash plus, but should settle in as an above-average offering. The change is inconsistent, looking average in some outings, below-average in others.

Hearn generally works off the fastball almost exclusively early in outings, before mixing in the secondaries more as he tries to turn over the lineup multiple times. And that's the open question here: Can Hearn work through a lineup multiple times as a starter? He tends not to hold his velocity deep in games, and the breaker can get rounded and slurvy as he tires as well. The command profile is a bit fringy; while he throws strikes generally, he can be wild within the zone. Hearn is exactly the type of prospect arm who may benefit from changing reliever roles. Where before he may have been either a frustrating starter with command and durability issues or a one-inning power arm, now he could be a multi-inning fireman or an "opener" as well. The stuff is also good enough to close.

The Risks: Moderate. I try to avoid throwing low risk on prospect arms who haven't already bagged a few major-league per diems, but Hearn could get outs in la grande liga with his fastball alone. His command issues require further ironing, but he doesn't need much more refinement to have a long career in the late innings, and there are those on staff who think I'm underselling his chances of becoming an effective starter.

Ben Carsley's Fantasy Take: In general I hate guys with Hearn's profile, but for a long time I've really loved Hearn. I wish he'd been traded, oh, almost anywhere else save for Colorado or Baltimore, as if he was a Padre or a Giant or something I might try to push Bret into sneaking him on to the end of the 101. Alas, Hearn is a Ranger, and that means we may actually want to root for him to move to the bullpen where he could earn some saves. If he stays in the rotation, the WHIP and ERA are likely to hurt too much for you to enjoy the strikeouts.

6. Cole Winn RHP
OFP: 60   Likely: 50   ETA: 2021
Born: 11/25/99   Age: 19   Bats: R   Throws: R   Height: 6'2"   Weight: 190
Origin: Round 1, 2018 Draft (#15 overall)

The Report: Winn isn't your typical first-round righty prep arm, as he doesn't have an overpowering fastball, and instead makes it work with pitchability and a relatively advanced arsenal. He's a plus athlete with a very smooth delivery and clean arm action to top it off.

Winn uses both a four-seamer and a two-seamer, and his fastballs sit from 90-94. He shows a plus 12-6 curveball with a high spin rate with plus depth and good feel in addition to a harder 85-86 slider with gloveside action and dive. He hasn't shown off his changeup much, but when he has it flashes average and should develop into a quality offering.

Winn's delivery and athleticism lead to a better command projection than most prep arms, and his current level of polish suggests he could move fairly quickly. With a four-pitch mix and an average command projection, Winn is a relatively safe bet to become a mainstay in an MLB rotation. Additionally, his well-rounded arsenal and fastball velocity give him a fall-back role as a late-inning bullpen arm if his changeup or command don't progress as expected.

The Risks: High. Even if he's not as risky as the usual prep arm, he's still a prep arm. Pitchers have higher rates of regression of stuff and injury than their position player counterparts and Winn's distance from the big leagues exacerbates the risk.

Ben Carsley's Fantasy Take: As a fan of the game you may enjoy pitchers who survive on pitch mix and command as much as pure stuff. As a fantasy player, you should be more interested in strikeouts. Winn has just enough upside that he's probably worth owning if your league holds 200 prospects, but those of you in shallower formats can drop him on your watch list for now.

7. Brock Burke   LHP

OFP: 55   Likely: 45   ETA: 2020
Born: 08/04/96   Age: 22   Bats: L   Throws: L   Height: 6'4"   Weight: 200
Origin: Round 3, 2014 Draft (#96 overall)

The Report: The "primary" piece in the deal for Jurickson Profar, the Rangers received another high minors arm that has helium going into the 2019 season. The tall athletic lefty has some extreme bend in his torso during the windup which results in a strange look for hitters, especially lefties, who can't pick up the ball until the actual release from an extreme over the top delivery that sees Burke falling off the mound to his gloveside and home plate. The result is a fastball that appears even faster than the 93-95 that he usually sits in games.

To go along with the fastball Burke mixes in an above average 79-80 curveball with 1 to 7 break, a slider that flashes average with average dive, and a below average 82-84 changeup that has some fade, but lacks significant tumble to get consistent whiffs.

Burke is able to stay within and around the zone well, but ultimately has below average command due to being unable to consistently hit spots with the fastball or changeup. When he tries to stay on the outside corner to righties and break the changeup off the plate, he regularly struggles to put it in a location where hitters are tempted. Due to the delivery's noise, it's hard to project much more command as Burke is already a quality athlete with strong limbs and body control.

Burke profiles as a back of the rotation starter who works off his plus 93-95 fastball and utilizes three different secondaries to get through a lineup multiple times. Without improvements to the changeup, Burke may be better suited to a bullpen role, where he could have his fastball play up even further. If Burke can take another step forward with the changeup like he did in 2018, a middle of the rotation spot isn't out of the question.

The Risks: With improved command and a better changeup in 2018, he increased the odds he'd be a productive member of an MLB rotation significantly. The changeup consistency still needs to improve before slotting into a rotation spot. If he stalls out where he is now, he should be able to find a home in a low-setup role where he can brutalize lefties with his fastball/breaking ball combo.

8. Joe Palumbo   LHP

OFP: 55   Likely: 45   ETA: 2019
Born: 10/26/94   Age: 24   Bats: L   Throws: L   Height: 6'1"   Weight: 168
Origin: Round 30, 2013 Draft (#910 overall)

The Report: Palumbo looked like a promising arm before tearing his UCL in 2017. After the requisite year-and-a-half away from the diamond, he returned to the mound last summer and alleviated many of the concerns evaluators had about his prospects for recovery.

Palumbo is 6-foot-1 with a high waist and long levers on a wiry frame. He is a quality athlete with controlled fluid movements and clean arm action. Palumbo sits 91-94 and tops out at 96 with a high spin rate, but his command of the pitch varies from average to below-average. His best secondary is a plus curveball with an excellent spin rate and plus depth, although his feel for it was inconsistent last summer. His low-80s changeup flashes average with good arm speed and deception with some tumble and armside action. The cambio is his most inconsistent offering, as he occasionally misses up and it can get him into trouble.

Many of Palumbo's current issues aren't surprising after TJS, as his command and feel can vary from inning to inning. His delivery is clean and he could improve his command as he gets further from surgery and adds weight to his slight frame. Currently, Palumbo projects as a back of the rotation starter or a setup arm depending on how his changeup develops. There's mid-rotation upside if his fastball command takes a step forward.

The Risks: Palumbo needs to take small steps forward in command and consistency with all three pitches to actualize. His delivery suggests better command is possible, but he still has to take those strides. Without such improvement, he may wind up in middle relief.

Ben Carsley's Fantasy Take: It's fine to keep Palumbo on your watch list in deep leagues since he figures to get a crack at MLB playing time at some point in 2019. That being said, Texas is among the worst places imaginable for a rookie pitcher, and there's no premium upside here. Basically, remember the name if you end up needing innings, but don't bank on him making super meaningful fantasy contributions.

9 Hans Crouse   RHP

OFP: 55   Likely: 45   ETA: 2021
Born: 09/15/98   Age: 20   Bats: L   Throws: R   Height: 6'4"   Weight: 180
Origin: Round 2, 2017 Draft (#66 overall)

The Report: Crouse is one of the most exciting arms in the system, thanks to three offerings that flash above-average or better, including a double-plus bender. The right-hander is a plus athlete with quick twitch and excellent control of his 6-foot-4 frame. He has a strong lower half with broad shoulders and room for more muscle throughout his torso.

Crouse's delivery is unorthodox and extremely rotational, and he fires from a cross-fire arm slot. He sits 94-96 and tops out at 98 with a high-spin four-seamer that features armside action, though that velocity dips late in games. He has a 70 breaking ball—he calls it a slider, pitch classification systems have their work cut out for them—and a good idea of how to use it. Crouse's mid-80s changeup was one of the early concerns with this profile, but it flashes above-average with quality deception and tumble and he seems to have improving feel for it. Combine it all and he has three separate offerings he can miss bats with.

Crouse currently has below-average command and it's hard to project too much more due to his loud, rotational delivery. The athleticism affords him more command than the motion would suggest and it's possible that it could improve further as he matures, though guys with his delivery and competent command are the exceptions, not the rule.

Crouse fits best in a one time through the order (OTTO) role where he can use his three-pitch mix to maximum effectiveness without suffering any velocity drop late in games. Alternatively, he could fit in a backend rotation spot where he pitches deep into starts on his good days while leaving early in his lesser outings. If he's able to enhance his command, he may even have No. 3 upside.

The Risks: Moderate. Crouse is relatively low-risk in one sense, in that his fastball/breaking ball mix give him a great chance to be productive in the pen in a single-inning role. The below-average command and lack of reliable command projection could keep him from sliding into a rotation spot or as a multi-innings reliever.

Ben Carsley's Fantasy Take: Red flags in his delivery and with his command profile abound, but I'd rather roll the dice on a guy like Crouse figuring it out than go with a lower-ceiling arm like Palumbo. Think of it this way: if Crouse clicks, you may not be able to replicate his production with a guy on the waiver wire. If Palumbo or either of the next two guys click, they'll still be fairly dime-a-dozen.

10 Tyler Phillips   RHP

OFP: 50   Likely: 40   ETA: 2021
Born: 10/27/97   Age: 21   Bats: R   Throws: R   Height: 6'5"   Weight: 200
Origin: Round 16, 2015 Draft (#468 overall)

The Report: Phillips is significantly thicker than his listed 200 pounds now, and he has the frame of a durable, innings-eating starter. The stuff is a bit light for the "No. 3 or late-inning reliever" prospect class, however. His velocity is averagish, although he will bump 95. It shows occasional run and sink, but gets a bit flat up, and the command isn't so good that it's rarely up.

Phillips will flash a downer, high-70s curve, but the shape is inconsistent. It can be a bit lazy and humpy at times, or look more like an 11-4 slurve. He can struggle to really sell the change, and it will get floaty or cut, though he'll flash a good one with sink and fade. The overall package can be fringy at times, but Phillips throws strikes and is comfortable mixing his pitches. Double-A will be a big test, but he is on track to crack the back of a rotation after a bit more seasoning.

The Risks: Moderate. No upper minors track record, lack of a clear out pitch, but relatively advanced arm who throws strikes.

Ben Carsley's Fantasy Take: Wrong profile, wrong organization, wrong-ish timeline.

The Next Five:

11

A.J. Alexy   RHP
Born: 04/21/98   Age: 21   Bats: R   Throws: R   Height: 6'4"   Weight: 217
Origin: Round 11, 2016 Draft (#341 overall)

The Report: In the 2018 Sally preview, I mentioned Alexy and Alex Speas as a pair of big-armed, high-bonused, projectable 2016 prep arms opening the season with Hickory. Speas pitched 28 2/3 IP out of the Hickory bullpen, alternating dominance with an inordinate amount of walks, and had Tommy John surgery in June; this is why you collect *all* the prep arms.

About as much went right for Alexy as went wrong for Speas. Last offseason, we talked up his projectability a lot, which is what you say for a cold-weather prep arm with a smooth delivery and the makings of a couple good pitches who hasn't done much yet. Now he's done more. The curveball that flashed plus occasionally now gets there pretty often. The fastball ticked up enough that we can no longer describe it as "fringy," and he was touching 97 repeatedly by the end of the season. He threw more strikes over the course of the year, and from June on he was one of the most dominant pitchers in the South Atlantic League. His changeup is behind the rest of the package, but that's true of all but the most precocious Low-A pitching prospect. If you're looking for a sleeper who is a few small improvements from shooting way up in the world, this might be your guy.

The Risks: A bit higher than Phillips. The curve gives him a better chance for an out pitch than Phillips, and would profile him better in relief if it comes to it; that's offset by a lower chance to stick in the rotation. Alexy has struggled in the past to throw strikes and that issue can obviously recur. We're going to need to see the change take another step here too. Still, he's already come a long way since the Darvish trade.

Ben Carsley's Fantasy Take: Wrong profile, wrong organization, wrong-ish timeline.

12 Charles Leblanc   3B
Born: 06/03/96   Age: 23   Bats: R   Throws: R   Height: 6'3"   Weight: 195
Origin: Round 4, 2016 Draft (#129 overall)

"Chuck The White" remains sneaky young for a 2016 college pick due to an oddball situation (his last year as a Quebec prep was technically a post-grad year) that saw him popped as a draft-eligible sophomore out of Pitt just a few days after his 20th birthday. Still just 22, he had an age-appropriate minor breakout in the Carolina League after we pegged him as a guy to watch last spring. He has a quick bat and knows what he wants to do in the box. He'll frequently get his money's worth swinging that quick bat and can get a little out of control, which leads to more swing-and-miss than you'd like for a guy with his polish. He spent most of the first half of the season at third and most of the second half at second, and he's athletic enough to profile at either position. He played both positions in the Arizona Fall League, but also added his first pro experience at first. He profiles as a potential regular at second or third, with a strong utility fallback if the bat winds up a bit short.

13 Jonathan Hernandez   RHP
Born: 07/06/96   Age: 22   Bats: R   Throws: R   Height: 6'2"   Weight: 175
Origin: International Free Agent, 2013

You could argue that Hernandez should be a bit higher on this list, but he tends to split evaluators, due to a rotational cross-fire delivery and the inconsistent fastball command that comes with it. That said, there's a lot to like in his profile. Hernandez is an athlete with good feel for his body and more ability to repeat his release point than most who pitch like he does. Hernandez throws a fastball that sits 96-98 with armside life, a hard 86-88 mph plus slider with sharp dive and gloveside movement, a high-70s curveball that flashes above-average with a big spin rate, and an above-average changeup with quality deception and tumble. The main problem lies in his fastball command, which often puts him behind in counts and makes it difficult for him to get to his bevy of secondaries. Hernandez appears to be a strong "pitch backwards" candidate and it would be interesting to see how effective he was on a team more comfortable with that pitching philosophy.

14 Mason Englert RHP
Born: 11/01/99   Age: 19   Bats: B   Throws: R   Height: 6'4"   Weight: 205
Origin: Round 4, 2018 Draft (#119 overall)

The overarching theme of this Rangers list is that the organization is "leaning into their strengths," so here we have a tall, athletic Texas prep arm who was pumping an easy 95 post-draft from a compact arm action. The #brand is strong. The Rangers went overslot in the fourth round, giving Englert one million smackers to buy him out of a Texas A&M commit. The fastball has run and sink, and he offers a full four-pitch mix at various stages of development. The slider is very projectable, and this is the exact type of profile Texas gets to jump in their first full pro season, so keep an eye out.

15 Pedro Gonzalez OF
Born: 10/27/97   Age: 21   Bats: R   Throws: R   Height: 6'5"   Weight: 190
Origin: International Free Agent, 2014

It seems appropriate that Gonzalez is now a Rangers prospect. The org has a type after all, so it's not a shock that Gonzalez was the player to be named later in the Lucroy deal. He's a toolsy center fielder (for now) with plus raw, a plus arm, and a potential plus glove in a corner. If Gonzalez does grow off center, there will be a lot of pressure on the bat to play to its full potential, and he is still a bit raw at the plate. It's a long and strong swing with just average bat speed, and he struggled to make consistent quality contact in the Sally. Our Rangers prospect lists from the last decade are littered with dudes with swing-and-miss issues in Hickory. But when they hit, they hit big.

The Injured Guys

Cole Ragans, LHP
The southpaw's season ended before it began, thanks to a UCL tear. Pre-injury Ragans was lauded as a bit of a Cole Hamels development kit, given his easy mechanics, clean arm action, a low-90s fastball, and a plus changeup that he had good feel for. Ragans did struggle with his command during the season, which is a common issue for pitchers who have problematic wear on their UCL, but he still managed to clean through hitters on the strength of his changeup. Before the injury, he was often mentioned as a pitcher who would likely be able to use fastball location, his changeup, and an average curveball to solidify himself into the middle of an MLB rotation. We'll just have to see how it all looks once he's back on the mound.

Chris Seise, SS
Seise missed the entire 2018 season due to shoulder surgery. The projection is still appealing though, as Seise has a premium build with athletic movements. Pre-surgery, Seise was seen as a good bet to be at least an average defender

at short due to his quick reactions and strong arm, but arm strength and consistency will be something to watch as he comes back. The bat is a bigger question, as his approach is still fairly raw. He has a big-leaguer's coordination and bat speed, but he'll need to find a way to tap into more of his average raw power while improving his patience and pitch recognition; if he can't, he'll be more of a utility guy than a starting SS.

Kyle Cody, RHP

Arguably the biggest disappointment for the Rangers came when Kyle Cody's partially strained UCL rehab turned into Tommy John surgery after a short rehab stint. Pre-injury Cody was making a major push up this list, and perhaps had a chance to work his way onto the 101 as well. Cody uses his 6-foot-7 frame to deliver a mid-high 90's fastball on an extreme downhill plane, a consistently plus curveball, and a developing changeup that was regularly flashing average during his breakout. At the very least, Cody appeared on track for a spot in the back of the Rangers rotation or as a late-inning reliever.

Unfortunately he's 24 and he will likely miss all of next season, which makes him hard to rank. He will likely be close to turning 26 the next time he takes the bump and two years removed from a start against age-appropriate competition. At that point the best option for the Rangers and Cody may be to have him work strictly fastball/curveball out of the pen to see what he can do there.

Others of note:

Sam Huff, C, Full-season-A Hickory

It also seems appropriate that the Rangers have a prospect who sounds like a Sun-Records-era Johnny Cash protagonist. Huff is a big dude with big raw and better defense behind the plate than you'd expect for a 20-year-old catcher listed at 6-foot-4, 230 lbs. But a swinging he will go, he will go, and that was an issue in his first taste of full-season ball. Despite his large frame, there are questions about his durability behind the plate, and he's playing more first base and DH at this point in his pro career than you'd like. So we have a good collection of tools, a chance to stick behind the plate, and another very Rangers prospect. Check back in when he kills a ball in Reno, just to watch it die.

Tyreque Reed, 1B, Full-season-A Hickory

Reed was drafted in the 8th round of the 2017 MLB draft out of Itawamba Community College, where he spent a season completely tearing through overmatched pitchers. At 6-foot-2, 260 pounds, Reed is about as large-bodied as large body first baseman come and he hits like it. He has plus bat speed and double-plus raw power, but he has little experience against quality competition. He struggled to pick up spin and off-speed early on in professional ball, but adjusted to put up gargantuan numbers down the stretch. In the second half of the season, Reed put up a .424 wOBA while maintaining a 10.8% walk rate with manageable strikeout numbers. The coordination and bat speed are both there to take advantage of his raw strength if he's able to continue improving against quality secondaries.

Jonathan Ornelas, SS, AZL Rangers

Pre-draft Ornelas was viewed primarily as a stereotypical toolsy athletic body who needed to be taught how to hit. In the AZL, he changed those perceptions quickly. He moves like a premium athlete with quick twitchy bursts and he has an instinctual feel for getting pop from his still-immature build. He generates plus bat speed and has quality bat-to-ball skills that allow him to make consistent contact on fastballs around the zone. Ornelas should be able to gain weight without losing foot speed or flexibility and he could develop above-average raw power. He's also fairly patient at the plate, as he walked 25 times in 203 plate appearances this summer.

Mike Matuella, RHP, Advanced-A Down East

This seems like a good time to point out that we don't use the 101 spot strictly for the 101st best prospect in baseball—it's more for a player we want to highlight or one we like better than anyone else. Regardless, Matuella didn't exactly reward our ranking in 2018. He struggled with his command before getting moved to the pen to manage his innings. He still has a plus fastball, and can touch higher. He's added a slider which he doesn't really have a feel for yet, and will still flash a power change. Matuella will be 25 next year and may never return to the starting rotation. We'll keep an eye on the stuff in 2019, because… well, we did like him more than anyone else, but for now he's yet another reason I still want to end every pitcher risk entry with: "Also, he's a pitcher."

Top Talents 25 and Under (born 4/1/93 or later):

1. Rougned Odor
2. Joey Gallo
3. Jose Leclerc
4. Nomar Mazara
5. Leody Taveras
6. Ronald Guzman
7. Bubba Thompson
8. Julio Pablo Martinez
9. Anderson Tejeda
10. Taylor Hearn

Texas Rangers 2019

The Rangers' 25 and under list features many of the names you're used to, including a young core of big-leaguers. Leading that group is Odor. Though Odor missed a significant amount of time at the beginning of the season due to a hamstring injury, he compiled 2.4 WARP and finished the year with a 97 DRC+ and a career-high 7.5 FRAA. After a rough 2017, Odor's rebound confirms that he's still an integral part of this Rangers roster.

Gallo again makes the list after having a similar-ish season to the previous one. You look at his numbers and think that maybe, just maybe, his hitting ability is sustainable. He had another 40 homer season, and even though his DRC+ dropped a bit, the dip wasn't alarming. He posted 2.7 WARP this season—lower than the 3.1 he put up in 2017—but a 2+ WARP player who can hit 40-something home runs is a good thing to have.

Jose Leclerc makes the list for the first time after coming off a very, very strong 2018. He posted a 2.87 DRA and also improved his walk and strikeout numbers considerably. After fanning 85 hitters in 58 innings, he'll return as the Rangers closer in 2019.

Dropping from first to fourth is Mazara. Mazara turns 24 in April, and is coming off another 20 home run season, one in which he raised his DRC+ to 98. Defensively, he produced the worst FRAA numbers of his career, though it's worth mentioning that he spent most of the season nursing a thumb injury. Mazara was the headliner of the Rangers 25 and under list the last two years, but after three seasons of middling production, it's getting harder to imagine him as a star. Perhaps this is just who he is as a major leaguer.

Sixth on the list is Ronald Guzmán, who made his debut in April. He's still young and hasn't reached his full potential. His walk and strikeout numbers are concerning, but he has time to adjust.

The remainder of the list features the toolsy "hey those guys might be good let's see what they can do" type of prospects this organization loves to cultivate. They didn't hit on a ton of those types in their last cycle—which is one of the reasons why Texas is looking up at their division mates from the AL West cellar.

Part 3: Featured Articles

The Hole in The Shift is Fixing Itself

Russell Carleton

I've been on a bit of a mission against The Shift of late. I'm not out to get The Shift for the usual reasons that people oppose it. The words "the right way to play the game" won't be found on my lips. If a team wants to pursue a strategy that is within the rules and it works, then by all means, they have my blessing (not that they need it). Instead, my concern with The Shift is a worry that it doesn't work, or at least that it has a flaw that needs fixing.

The data show that while The Shift does a decent job of preventing singles on balls in play (what it's supposed to do), it also increases the number of walks that happen in front of it, and the number of additional walks outweighs the number of singles saved. It's a problem because you can't throw a guy out if he gets to walk to first base.

But the "why" was important. It seemed that The Shift was changing the way in which pitchers pitched. We saw that there were fewer fastballs thrown in front of The Shift than we might otherwise expect, and that pitchers tended to stay out of the strike zone a little more. Not by a lot. In fact, it might not even be visible to the naked eye. The percentage of pitches that are out of the zone goes from 51.0 to 53.3 from a standard defense (two right/two left) to a full shift (three on one side). That difference stands up even after we control for the types of hitters that get shifted against. And it's enough to drive up the walk rate to where it cancels out the benefits that teams thought they were getting with The Shift… and then some.

But there was some hope. I found that when individual pitchers stayed closer to the in-zone/out-of-zone mix that they used without The Shift on, they could still get the benefits of The Shift without the walk problems. So, in theory, a team could simply figure out a way to convince its pitchers to not fall prey to the walk trap and The Shift would once again be their friend.

It's reasonable to think that some teams might be more hip to this idea than others. Maybe some figured it out a year before the others. Maybe they were better at getting the message across to their pitchers. Or, maybe no one has figured it out yet.

Warning! Gory Mathematical Details Ahead!

I used data from 2015-2017, made available through MLB's data portal, Baseball Savant. They are kind enough to note when teams are using an infield shift (three fielders on one side of second base), as opposed to a "strategic shift" (someone's playing a bit out of position, but it's not quite that drastic) or a "standard" alignment.

Since we're doing this by team, I can't just look at raw walk rates, because we know that some teams have good pitchers and others have not-so-good pitchers. Some have a mix of both. I used the log-odds ratio method to take into account a batter's general walking proclivities, and a pitcher's as well, and then shoving them into a binary logistic regression. Then, I asked the computer to generate a specific coefficient for each team's pitchers, for when they went into The Shift and how that affected their walk rate.

Using those coefficients, I was able to project what would happen if a league-average pitcher faced a league-average hitter (which we expect would product a league-average walk rate; from 2015-2017, 7.7 percent of plate appearances ended in a walk) and then just switched his hat. Here's the top five and the bottom five:

Top 5 Teams	Projected Shift Walk Rate	Bottom 5 Teams	Projected Shift Walk Rate
Rockies	6.2%	Rangers	11.2%
Pirates	6.7%	Mets	10.4%
Indians	7.2%	Dodgers	10.2%
Astros	7.3%	Cardinals	9.9%
Braves	7.7%	Tigers	9.7%

There are probably people out there right now trying to figure out what the common thread is among the top and bottom teams. I'm sure, because this is Baseball Prospectus, people are already trying to make the case that sabermetric "early adopters" have some sort of edge here. I think that the more interesting piece is that by the time you get to fifth place in The Shift, we're at league average.

As a sanity check, I examined the issue on a pitch-by-pitch level, looking at how often pitchers threw their pitches in the GameDay strike zone, and again using the same basic methodology and getting team-specific coefficients. The names on the list re-arranged themselves, but the idea was the same, and the two lists correlated with an R of .593.

There's a reason that I don't usually do this type of leaderboard post. I don't really know what the Rockies, Pirates, Indians, Astros, and Braves have in common, or what they have that the bottom five don't. I can put a shrug emoji here and say, "Well, it must be something!" but that seems like a cop-out. Instead, I'd like to present another table and suggest that the table above doesn't even really matter anymore.

Year	League Percent Outside K Zone (Full Shift)	League Percent in K Zone (No Shift)	Difference
2015	54.1%	51.1%	3.0%
2016	53.3%	50.9%	2.4%
2017	52.6%	50.9%	1.7%
2018	52.0%	50.7%	1.3%

The hole in The Shift is fixing itself, and it's coming down really fast league wide. In my earlier work on The Shift, I suggested that until teams stopped having such a huge difference between their out-of-zone rate with and without The Shift on, there would just be too many walks for The Shift to make sense. It seems that all 30 of them have been working toward just that. I once estimated that it takes about 10 years for an idea to filter its way through baseball. At this rate, it looks like teams are going to catch up a lot faster than that. And yeah, they're all saber-smart now.

It's likely that whatever magic it was that the Rockies and Pirates had has made its way to Texas and Queens. Or is at least on its way. And if teams are committing to fixing the walk problem, then it's likely that they will continue shifting and shifting a lot.

And eventually it's going to actually make sense for them to do it.

—*Russell Carleton is a former author of Baseball Prospectus and now an analyst for the New York Mets.*

The State of the Quality Start

Rob Mains

One of the seven things you (probably) didn't know about the 2018 season is that quality starts—defined as a start lasting six or more innings with three or fewer earned runs allowed—as a percentage of total starts cratered to an all-time low of 41 percent. I want to look a little more deeply into this, since it's been a while (May of 2016, to be exact) since I've examined quality starts.

The term *quality start* is credited to *Philadelphia Inquirer* sportswriter John Lowe. It's been derided ever since he coined it in December of 1985. Three runs in six innings? That's a 4.50 ERA! In what world is that a measure of quality?

Let's start with that criticism. It's true that 3 x 9 / 6 = 4.5. (You came here for this sort of high-level math, right?) But it's also true that type of start, meeting the bare minimum for earning a quality start, is unusual. Here's the proportion of quality starts in which the pitcher lasted exactly six innings and yielded exactly three earned runs. (I'm going to confine this analysis to the 30-team era, 1998-present. Almost all data retrieved in this article is via the Baseball-Reference Play Index.)

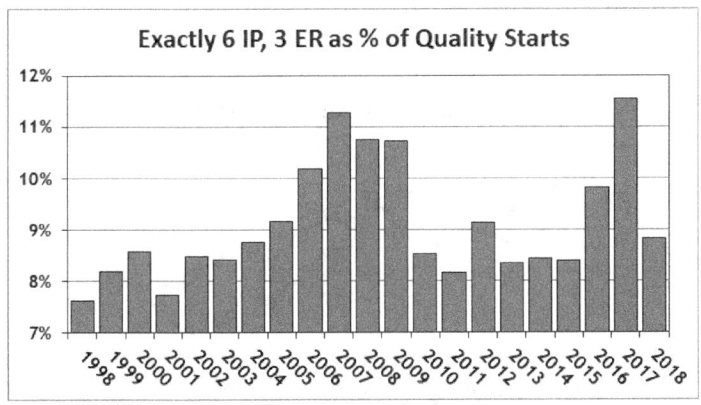

There were 1,997 quality starts in 2018. Only 176, or fewer than one in 11, featured a pitcher going six innings and allowing three earned runs. Put another way, the percentage of quality starts that resulted in a 4.50 ERA (8.8 percent) is less than half the percentage of games in which a batter hit two home runs and his team lost (22.5 percent; 237-69 won-lost). That doesn't impugn hitting two homers.

So if a 4.50 ERA isn't the norm, what is? How good are quality starts? Pretty good, it turns out. First, on a team level:

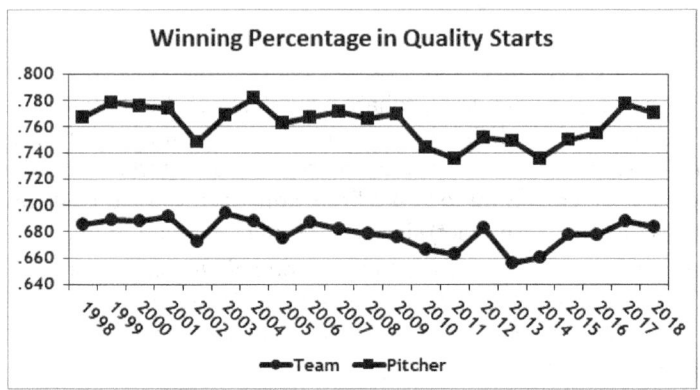

Teams receiving a quality start from their pitcher won 68.4 percent of their games in 2018, in line with the 30-team era average of 67.9 percent. A team with a .684 winning percentage wins 111 games. Getting a quality start is definitely a good thing. Individual pitchers throwing quality starts have a higher winning percentage because a big slice of team losses is assigned to a reliever.

If teams do well in quality starts, how well do the starting pitchers do? Again, very well.

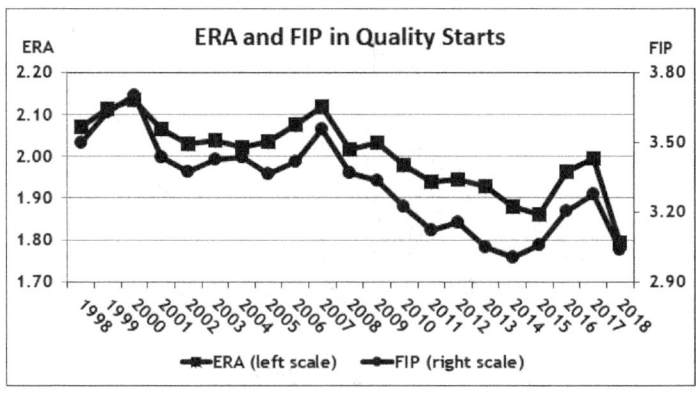

Pitchers in quality starts had a 1.79 ERA (blue line) in 2018, *the lowest in the 30-team era*. Their FIP was higher, 3.04, but still excellent. In the 30-team era, only 2014 had a lower FIP for quality starts, 3.01.

But, of course, the run environment in 2014 was different. Teams in 2014 scored 4.07 runs per game, the fewest in a non-strike year since 1976. They scored 4.45 runs per game in 2018. So surrendering a 3.04 FIP in 2018 is more impressive than 3.01 in 2014. Accordingly, let's look at ERA and FIP in quality starts relative to league averages.

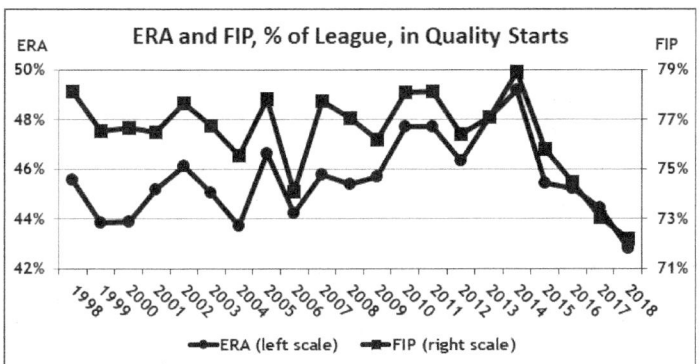

This tells a more dramatic story. Starting pitchers in 2018 gave up a 4.19 ERA and a 4.21 FIP. Starters in quality starts gave up a 1.79 ERA, 43 percent of the league average. Starters in quality starts gave up a 3.04 FIP, 72 percent of the league average. Both of these marks represent lows in the 30-team era.

The takeaway here is this: *Quality starts are better, relative to other starts, than they've ever been over the past 21 years.*

Maybe during the winter I'll look at this over a longer arc of time. For now, though, we can definitively say quality starts are the best they've ever been since the Diamondbacks and Rays joined the majors.

Yet, paradoxically, they're down.

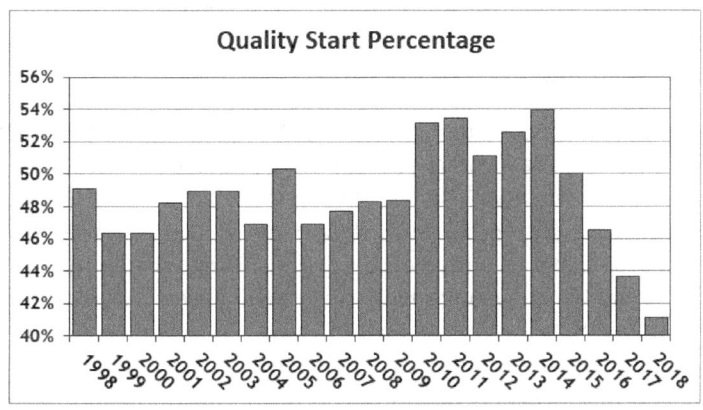

This graph covers only the 30-team era. In my article last week, though, I looked at the years 1908-2018. The result was the same. The 41 percent of starts in 2018 that were quality starts are an all-time low, well below the runners-up: 1930's 43 percent (the year teams scored an all-time record 5.55 runs per game) and last year's 44 percent.

The normal explanation for a dip in quality start percentage is an increase in scoring. When teams score a lot of runs, it's harder for starting pitchers to last six or more innings and limit opponents to three earned runs. From 1998 to 2014, the correlation between runs scored per game and the percentage of starts that were quality starts was -0.94. That means there was an extremely close relationship: More runs, fewer quality starts. Too small a sample? Go back to the start of the Expansion Era, 1961, and the relationship is even more negative, a -0.95 correlation, though 2014.

But that's broken down over the past four years:

- 2015: Runs per game increased from 4.07 to 4.25, quality start percentage decreased from 54.0 to 50.1. Yes, that's a negative relationship, but the regression model would predict a decline of 1.5 percentage points. We got 3.9 instead.
- 2016: Runs per game increased from 4.25 to 4.48, quality start percentage decreased from 50.1 to 46.6. Past experience would suggest a decline of just 1.8 percentage points. We got 3.4.
- 2017: Runs per game increased from 4.48 to 4.65, quality start percentage decreased from 46.6 to 43.6. Again, the direction's right, but the magnitude isn't. Using the relationship from 1998 to 2014, that increase in scoring should've reduced quality starts by 1.3 percentage points, not 2.9.
- 2018: Runs per game declined from 4.65 to 4.45. That should've resulted in the quality start percentage moving in the other direction, rising 1.6 points. It didn't. It fell 2.6 points, as noted, to an all-time low.

Granted, we're talking about just four years here. Maybe they're outliers. But I don't think they are. Quality starts, as noted, are as good or better than ever. But they're rarer than ever as well. And I think I know why.

To get a quality start, you need to allow three or fewer earned and pitch at least six innings. That's 18 outs. Here's a graph showing the number of starting pitchers who limited their opponents to three or fewer earned runs but got pulled after pitching at least five innings but fewer than six:

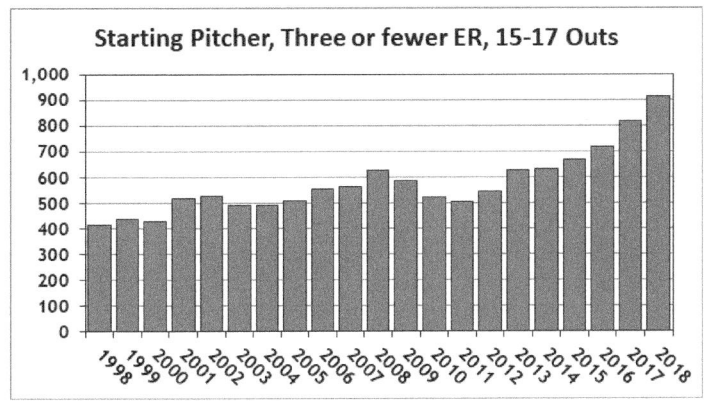

A pitcher getting 15 outs pitched five innings. A pitcher getting 16 outs pitched 5 1/3. A pitcher getting 17 outs pitched 5 2/3. More than ever before, pitchers are being removed from games in which they are within 1-3 outs of a quality start, falling just short of the six-inning finish line. Widespread acknowledgement of the times-through-the-order penalty and a flotilla of available bullpen arms is making the quality start simultaneously both more excellent and more rare.

Which is ironic, given that we saw a new post-war quality start record this season:

Rank	Pitcher	Season	Consecutive QS
1	Jacob deGrom	2018	24
2	Bob Gibson	1968	22
-	Chris Carpenter	2005	22
4	Johan Santana	2004	21
5	Luis Tiant	1968	20
-	Mike Scott	1986	20
-	Jake Arrieta	2015	20
8	Robin Roberts	1952	19
-	Tom Seaver	1973	19
-	Jack Morris	1983	19
-	Greg Maddux	1998	19
-	Josh Johnson	2010	19
-	Jon Lester	2014	19

While there have been longer streaks spread over multiple seasons, no pitcher since World War II threw more consecutive quality starts in one year than Jacob deGrom this year. The fact that he did in a year in which quality starts were the rarest they've ever been adds to the accomplishment.

—Rob Mains is an author of Baseball Prospectus.

Heads-Up Hacking—The First Pitch

Matthew Trueblood

Batters fell behind in a higher percentage of all plate appearances in 2018 than in any previous season for which we have pitch-by-pitch data. That kind of granular information goes back only to 1988, but we might safely assume (given all we know about baseball as it had been before that, and as it has been in the years since) that batters have *never* fallen behind at a higher rate than they did last season.

Through the 1990s, the percentage of all plate appearances that began 0-1 hovered in the high 30s and low 40s. In the 2000s, it rose steadily but slowly, through the mid-40s. In 2018, 49.8 percent of all trips to the plate began 0-1. That, as much as anything, captures in microcosm the nature of hitting in MLB today.

A countdown clock toward strike three begins ticking almost the moment a batter takes his place in the box. The league's adjusted OPS+ on the first pitch was higher in 2018 than ever before, and that has been true in most of the last 10 seasons. Batters hit .264/.289/.442 in all plate appearances in which they swung at the first pitch last season, and .241/.330/.395 in all plate appearances in which they took that first offering.

The percentage differences in batting average and isolated power there favor swinging at the first pitch by more than in any season since 1988, while the difference in on-base percentage favors taking by more than ever. If you want to get on base at a decent clip, it's a good idea to be patient, but you run the risk of missing the only chances you'll get to produce power.

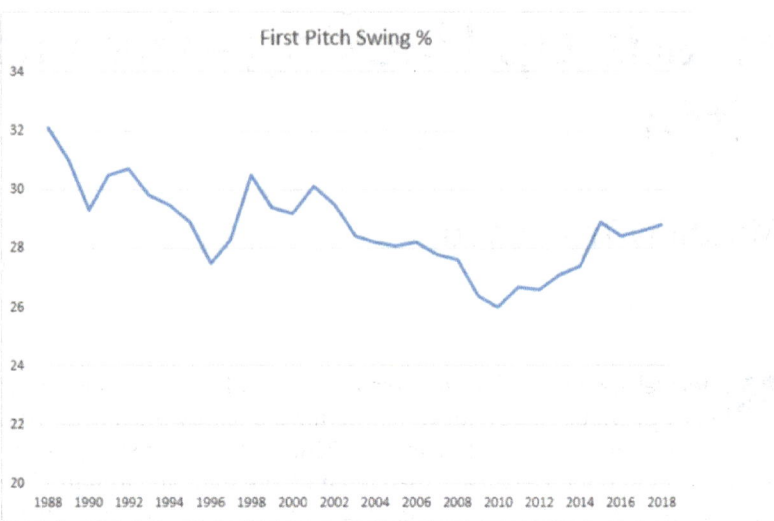

The league swung at the first pitch 28.8 percent of the time in 2018. With the isolated exception of 2015, that's the highest that number has climbed since 2002, but it might not be high enough. With the help of BP research maven Rob McQuown, I looked at the aggregate Called Strike Probability (CSProb) on the first pitch for each season since 2008, when the implementation of PITCHf/x first made measuring that possible. It's risen sharply during that period.

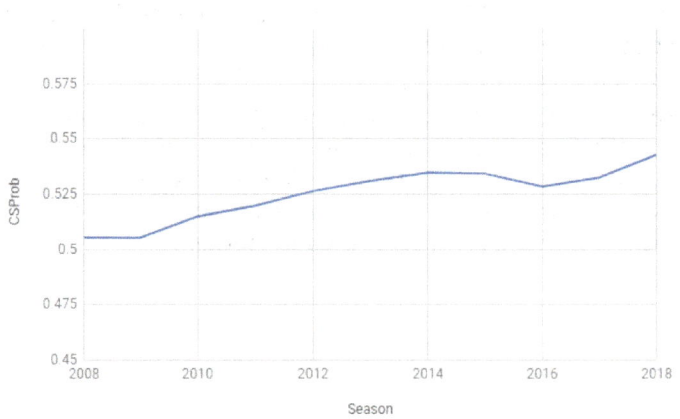

Called Strike Probability, First Pitch of PA (2008-2018)

Called Strike Probability is exactly what it sounds like: a pitch with a given CSProb has roughly that chance of being called a strike, if not swung at. In 2018, a batter who took 100 first pitches from a random sampling of the league's pitchers might expect to fall behind 54 or 55 times—up from 50 or 51 times in 2008. Almost regardless of pitch type (and, notably, especially in the case of fastballs), the first pitch tends to have more of the zone right now than ever before.

Pitchers are better at throwing strikes. They have better stuff, and believe more in their ability to miss bats within the zone. Perhaps most importantly, they know that batters are looking for one thing on the first pitch: a fastball. If they don't get it, they're likely to take the pitch. Check out how the use of sinkers and four-seamers on the first pitch has changed in a decade:

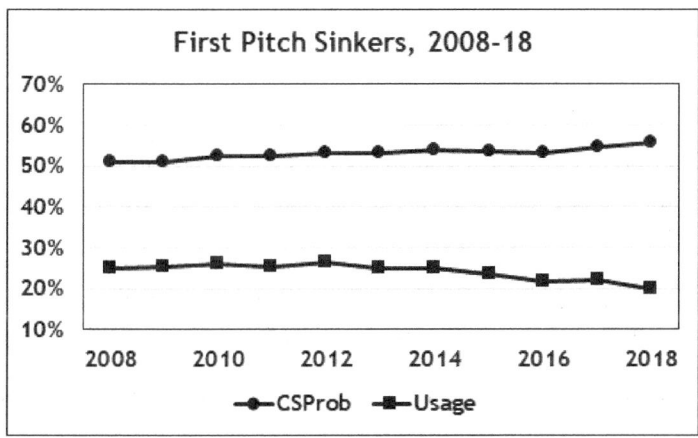

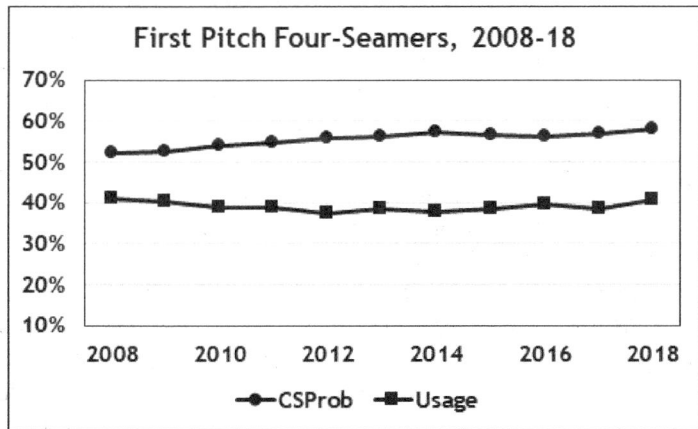

The sinker is losing its place in baseball, but the rate at which pitchers have thrown it on the first pitch hasn't dropped any faster than its usage rate in other counts. Pitchers have actually gone to their four-seamer *more* often to open counts, in the last few years, after a dip in the 2012-2015 period. What's really changed, though, and what shows up in both charts above, is that pitchers are catching more of the zone with first-pitch fastballs than they were a decade ago, or a half-decade ago. They're attacking right away, even with the pitch they know batters are expecting. The message is pretty clear: batters are being too passive.

Sliders, curves, and changeups each have more of the zone when thrown on the first pitch than they did several years ago, too, though the effect is less pronounced. Pitchers have seen the numbers; they know batters are doing better on the first pitch itself. They still feel safe throwing more and better strikes than ever before, figuring they'll come out ahead as long as they keep getting ahead to open each battle.

The Moneyball revolution brought an increased league-wide focus on OBP, which resulted in a de facto mandate to take a more patient tack at the plate. It worked very well for a while, as batters with poor plate discipline were compelled to either adjust or be expelled from the league, and pitchers with poor control were slowly weeded out.

However, concurrent with that revolution, and spurred by it in some ways, was the evolution of the pitching paradigm that now dominates the game. As batters ratcheted up their focus on inflating pitch counts and working walks, pitchers honed theirs on throwing strikes and missing bats. The league's understanding of what makes a good pitcher improved at least as much, from the mid-1990s through the mid-2000s, as its understanding of what makes a good hitter. As amphetamines and other performance-enhancing drugs were phased mostly out of the game, and as PITCHf/x broke onto the scene, individuals and teams learned how to exploit the evolved approaches of even the smartest hitters.

The ability to avoid making outs is still the most valuable one in baseball, but the magnitude of its eclipse of slugging is smaller than ever. To a greater extent than power, on-base skills derive their value from chaining—from the on-base skill levels of the players on either side of a given individual. Eleven years ago, when the housing crisis hit, people learned the hard way that the value of their homes depended a good deal on the values of their neighbors' homes. The same wasn't true, though, of their cars. So it is now, with OBP and SLG.

The global OBP in 2018 was .318. The only seasons since the Dead Ball Era in which the league got on base at a worse clip were 2013-2015, 1988, 1971-1972, and 1963-1968. This is all happening despite the aforementioned evolution of the science of hitting. It's happening despite a shift in approach and focus, one that would steer OBP ever higher, if only it were working.

Instead, it's sitting at a low ebb, and while it does so, even guys who get on base often are a little less helpful than they were 10 years ago—or 20, or 40, or 60, or 70, or 80, or 90. They're less helpful, that is, because unless there happen to be three or four other guys in the lineup who get on just as regularly, their contribution is merely to forestall the inevitable. Runs happen, increasingly, when a sudden bang happens, and that means attacking early in the count—because pitchers are sure as hell doing that.

In a league making contact on barely 75 percent of its swings, and a league in which an increasing number of pitchers can throw multiple off-speed pitches for strikes in any count, the only way to consistently generate offense is going to be aggressive. This isn't necessarily true for individuals, like Mookie Betts and Jose Ramirez, who make a lot of contact and have excellent plate discipline, and whose power comes from such natural quickness in a short stroke. Most players have to make tradeoffs, though, whether it be lowering their contact rate or raising their chase rate, in order to consistently make the quality of contact necessary to survive in today's game.

Highest %	Lowest %
Javier Baez – 48.3	Joe Mauer – 4.6
Freddie Freeman – 47.1	Mookie Betts – 9.7
Ozzie Albies – 46.3	Brett Gardner – 10.7
Jose Altuve – 44.2	Jose Ramirez – 12.0
Nick Castellanos – 44.1	Jason Kipnis – 13.8
Joey Gallo – 42.3	Jesus Aguilar – 14.5
Corey Dickerson – 40.9	Xander Bogaerts – 15.8
Salvador Perez – 40.8	Brian Dozier – 16.3
Eddie Rosario – 40.7	Mike Trout – 17.6
Nick Ahmed – 40.4	Yasmani Grandal – 17.6

Top 10 and Bottom 10 Hitters, First-Pitch Swing Rate (2018)

The question isn't which of these lists one prefers, but what they each convey, qualitatively, about the cat-and-mouse game of early-count hitting. Those top five on the left, especially, drive home the fact that for most players, getting aggressive early in the count is now key to keeping strikeout rate down and hitting for power.

For now, the message is: pitchers are coming right after batters with the nastiest stuff they've ever had. Batters had better stop giving away strike one and force hurlers to adjust, or the global OBP crisis is only going to get worse.

—*Matthew Trueblood is an author of Baseball Prospectus.*

A Hymn for the Index Stat

Patrick Dubuque

We survived without computers. I know this, because I remember the day when my dad hooked up his brand-new Atari 400 computer to the back of our 12-inch Magnavox television, and the perfect blue of the memo pad lit up for the first time. I was born just on the edge of that transitional generation, of learning cursive and balancing checkbooks and just doing math all the time, constant manual arithmetic.

It still amazes me. We learned how to sail ships without computers. We learned how to do calculus. We built towers that didn't fall down, most of the time. We engineered catapults to knock them down anyway. We built a robust system of philosophy called "utilitarianism," founded on the principle that the good of an action is evaluated by summing the effects of that action, which is the kind of formula that would make the world's mainframes crash. The whole foundation of statistics as a field is "here's math you could easily do but would die of old age first."

The fact of the matter is that there is too much math in the world to do. There are too many things changing, and too many things too small to notice, for us to handle. At some point, they become too much for the computers to handle as well, which is why we have chaos theory and undetectable earthquakes, but it's not an even fight. At some point, we fall back on intuition, and given how under-equipped we are, we're forced to bestow that intuition with some sort of supernatural superiority, the "gut feeling," that we can't prove because we can only intuit that our intuition is better.

We're all lousy at intuition, and wonderful at lying to ourselves about it. The honest truth is that computers are far better at intuition than we are, because in order to know what feels "off" you have to know what's "on." In order to do that you have to constantly reassess the average of everything, then re-rank your own experience against it.

Test your own, by comparing these three anonymous lines:

Player	G	HR	AVG	OBP	SLG
Player A	156	38	.259	.342	.535
Player B	154	38	.280	.348	.527
Player C	158	38	.266	.343	.509

These all seem like pretty similar players, right? The second one a touch more batted-ball dependent, the third a little less strong, but all pretty good hitters. And you'd be right, about the latter. Not the former.

Here's the breakdown:

- Player A: 1991 Howard Johnson, 141 DRC+
- Player B: 1996 Dean Palmer, 121 DRC+
- Player C: 2018 Giancarlo Stanton, 114 DRC+

Baseball is fortunate to have escaped the seismic shifts of so many other sports, where the talents and performances of other eras are nearly unrecognizable. (And not just other sports: try to explain the greatness of the movie Duck Soup without adjusting for era.) But they're still there, and they're nearly impossible to account for manually, without having to resort to sweeping generalizations like "steroid era" or juiced-ball era" to throw out entire swathes of production.

This is all to say that we should celebrate the index stat, that simple 100-based scale with such a humble aim: just to give context. It's hard to imagine how we lived without them for so long. Sabermetricians have always tried to make their stats look like other stats: True Average mapped to batting average, FIP molded to look like and compare to ERA. It's easy to understand the motivation—these statistics carry an emotional value in them that is hard to resist, as with the .300 hitter and the 2.00 ERA—but even they fall prey to the same loss of scale as their unadjusted counterparts. If a .300 average means different things in different years, does that hold true for a .300 True Average?

Instead, 100 doesn't say anything, except above average or below. And it does it instantly, for every season in every run environment for any statistic we want it to. We should have more index stats: K%+, so we can stop comparing Mike Clevinger's career 9.46 K/9 to Nolan Ryan's 9.55. HBP%+, so we can note that Ron Hunt was getting plunked when nobody else was getting plunked, as opposed to that imitator Brandon Guyer. Some might note how stale these references are and accuse league-adjustment as a backward-looking drive, and this is true. But we're always looking backward, always comparing the new with the expectations already set. The index stat just forces us to be honest.

There's always resistance to a new statistic, especially one so outwardly simple and so internally complex. We tend to stick with what we know, even in the case of formulas that are supposed to tell us what we know. But if your resistance is that it seems too complicated, too counterintuitive, too "black boxy," I encourage you to consider why you feel that way. Because the real world is infinitely more complicated than baseball, where all the pitches go in one basic direction and the baserunners are only allowed to travel in four directions. Baseball statistics based on mixed methodology are almost impossibly intricate. So are skyscrapers and automobiles. That's why we have computers—to take the guesswork out of them.

—*Patrick Dubuque is an author of Baseball Prospectus.*

Index of Names

Alexy, A.J. 97, 109
Andrus, Elvis 18
Bandy, Jett 80
Beras, Jairo 87
Bird, Kyle 97
Burke, Brock 97, 106
Bush, Matt 50
Cabrera, Asdrubal 20
Calhoun, Willie 22
Chavez, Jesse 52
Chirinos, Michael 95
Choo, Shin-Soo 24
Crouse, Hans 88, 108
Curtis, Zac 97
d'Arnaud, Chase 95
Davidson, Matt 26
Del Pozo, Miguel 97
DeShields, Delino 28
Englert, Mason 111
Farrell, Luke 97
Forsythe, Logan 30
Gallo, Joey 32
Gardewine, Nick 97
Gomez, Jeanmar 97
Gonzalez, Pedro 81, 111
Granite, Zack 95
Guerrieri, Taylor 54
Guzman, Ronald 34
Hammel, Jason 56
Hearn, Taylor 89, 104
Heineman, Scott 82
Hernandez, Jonathan 90, 110
Huang, Wei-Chieh 91
Huff, Sam 95, 112
Jenkins, Eric 95
Jurado, Ariel 58
Kelley, Shawn 60
Kiner-Falefa, Isiah 36
Leblanc, Charles 110
Leclerc, Jose 62
Lynn, Lance 64
Martin, Brett 97
Martin, Chris 66
Martinez, Julio Pablo 83, 103
Mathis, Jeff 38
Matuella, Mike 92, 113
Mazara, Nomar 40
McAllister, Zach 97
Mendez, Yohander 68
Miller, Shelby 70
Minor, Mike 72
Moore, Adam 95
Odor, Rougned 42
Ornelas, Jonathan 95, 113
Pacheco, Sergio 97
Palumbo, Joe 93, 107
Pelham, C.D. 74
Pence, Hunter 44
Phillips, Tyler 94, 108
Reed, Tyreque 112
Sadzeck, Connor 97
Sampson, Adrian 76

Smyly, Drew	95	Tocci, Carlos	46
Speas, Alex	97	Trevino, Jose	86
Springs, Jeffrey	78	White, Eli	95
Taveras, Leody	84, 101	Winn, Cole	105
Tejeda, Anderson	95, 103	Wisdom, Patrick	48
Thompson, Bubba	85, 102		

Ballpark diagrams for Baseball Prospectus are created by THIRTY81Project, a design concept offering original ballpark artwork, including the new 'Ballparks of 2019' 11 x 17 color print.

Visit **www.thirty81project.com** for full details.

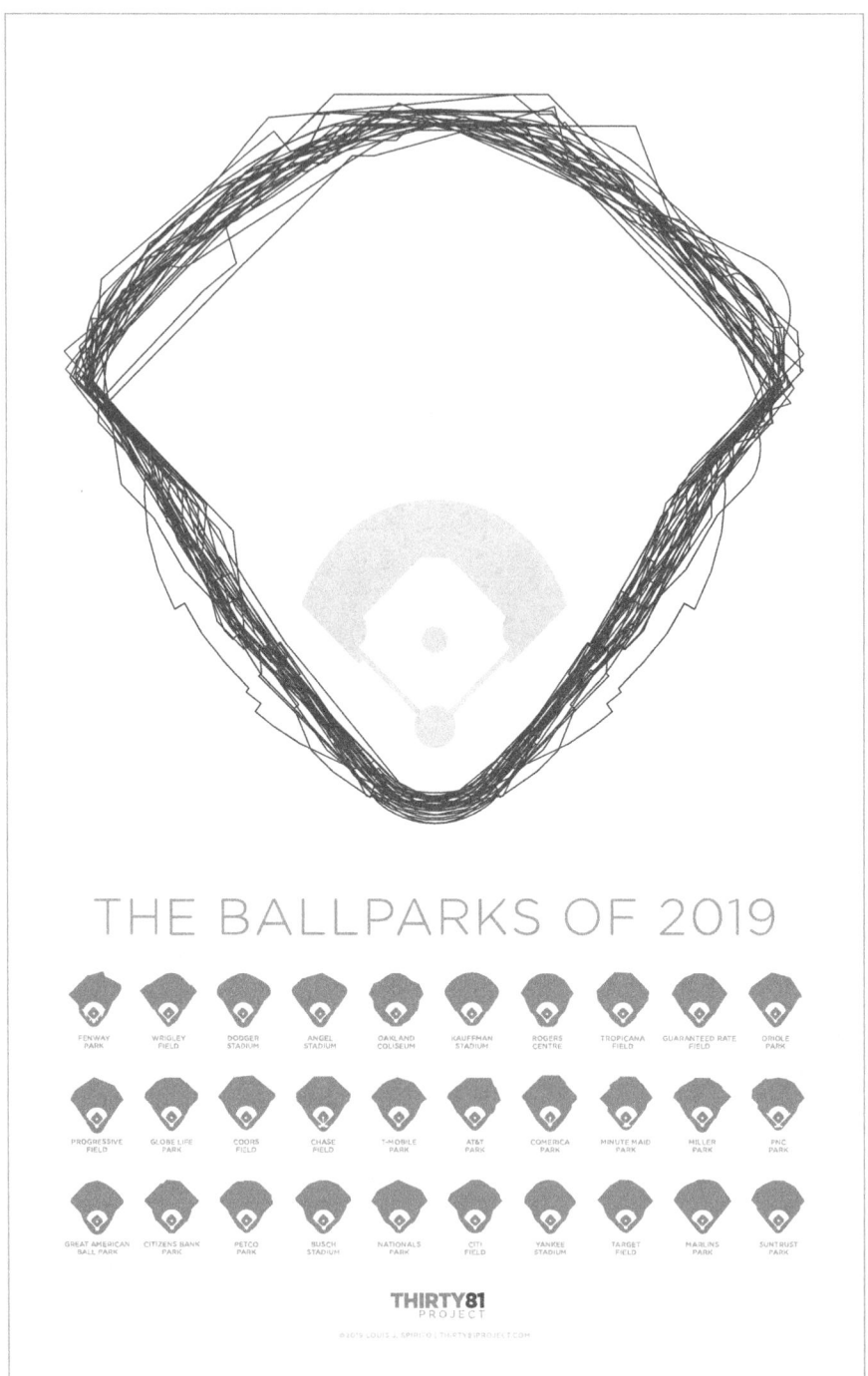